ETHICAL AND RELIGIOUS CLASSICS OF EAST AND WEST

Volume 1

THE BUDDHA, THE PROPHET AND THE CHRIST

THE BUDDHA, THE PROPHET AND THE CHRIST

F. H. HILLIARD

LONDON AND NEW YORK

First published in Great Britain in 1956 by George Allen & Unwin Ltd.

This edition first published in 2022
by Routledge
2 Park Square, Milton Park, Abingdon, Oxon OX14 4RN

and by Routledge
605 Third Avenue, New York, NY 10158

Routledge is an imprint of the Taylor & Francis Group, an informa business

© 1956 F. H. Hilliard

All rights reserved. No part of this book may be reprinted or reproduced or utilised in any form or by any electronic, mechanical, or other means, now known or hereafter invented, including photocopying and recording, or in any information storage or retrieval system, without permission in writing from the publishers.

Trademark notice: Product or corporate names may be trademarks or registered trademarks, and are used only for identification and explanation without intent to infringe.

British Library Cataloguing in Publication Data
A catalogue record for this book is available from the British Library

ISBN: 978-1-03-213267-9 (Set)
ISBN: 978-1-00-324156-0 (Set) (ebk)
ISBN: 978-1-03-214045-2 (Volume 1) (hbk)
ISBN: 978-1-03-214055-1 (Volume 1) (pbk)
ISBN: 978-1-00-323210-0 (Volume 1) (ebk)

DOI: 10.4324/9781003232100

Publisher's Note
The publisher has gone to great lengths to ensure the quality of this reprint but points out that some imperfections in the original copies may be apparent.

Disclaimer
The publisher has made every effort to trace copyright holders and would welcome correspondence from those they have been unable to trace.

THE BUDDHA
THE PROPHET
AND
THE CHRIST

by

F. H. HILLIARD

PH.D., B.D. (Lond.)

LONDON: GEORGE ALLEN & UNWIN LTD
NEW YORK: THE MACMILLAN COMPANY

First published in 1956

This book is copyright under the Berne Convention. Apart from any fair dealing for the purposes of private study, research, criticism or review, as permitted under the Copyright Act 1911, *no portion may be reproduced by any process without written permission. Enquiry should be made to the publishers*

*Printed in Great Britain
by C. Tinling & Co. Ltd.
Liverpool, London and Prescot.*

GENERAL INTRODUCTION

AS A RESULT of two Wars that have devastated the World men and women everywhere feel a twofold need. We need a deeper understanding and appreciation of other peoples and their civilizations, especially their moral and spiritual achievements. And we need a wider vision of the Universe, a clearer insight into the fundamentals of ethics and religion. How ought men to behave? How ought nations? Does God exist? What is His Nature? How is He related to His creation? Especially, how can man approach Him? In other words, there is a general desire to know what the greatest minds, whether of East or West, have thought and said about the Truth of God and of the beings who (as most of them hold) have sprung from Him, live by Him, and return to Him.

It is the object of this Series, which originated among a group of Oxford men and their friends, to place the chief ethical and religious masterpieces of the world, both Christian and non-Christian, within easy reach of the intelligent reader who is not necessarily an expert—the ex-Service man who is interested in the East, the undergraduate, the adult student, the intelligent public generally. The Series will contain books of three kinds: translations, reproductions of ideal and religious art, and background books showing the surroundings in which the literature and art arose and developed. These books overlap each other. Religious art, both in East and West, often illustrates a religious text, and in suitable cases the text and the pictures will be printed together to complete each other. The background books will often consist largely of translations. The volumes will be prepared by scholars of distinction, who will try to make them, not only scholarly, but intelligible and enjoyable. This Introduction represents the views of the General Editors as to the scope of the Series, but not necessarily the views of all contributors to it. The contents of the books will also be very varied—ethical and social, biographical, devotional, philosophic and mystical, whether in poetry, in pictures or in prose. There is a great wealth of material. Confucius lived in a time much like our own, when State was at war with State and the people suffering and disillusioned; and the 'Classics' he preserved or inspired show the social virtues that may unite families, classes and States into one great family, in obedience to the Will of Heaven. Asoka and Akbar (both of them great patrons of art) ruled a vast Empire on the principles of religious faith. There are the moral anecdotes and moral maxims of the Jewish and Muslim writers of the Middle Ages. There are the beautiful tales of courage, love and fidelity in the Indian and Persian epics. Shakespeare's plays show that he thought the true relation between man and man is love. Here and there a volume will illustrate the unethical or less ethical man and difficulties that beset him.

Then there are the devotional and philosophic works. The lives and legends (legends often express religious truth with clarity and beauty) of the Buddha, of the parents of Mary, of Francis of Assisi, and the exquisite sculptures and paintings that illustrate them. Indian and Christian religious music, and the words of prayer and praise which the music intensifies. There are the prophets and apocalyptic writers, Zarathustrian and Hebrew; the Greek philosophers, Christian thinkers—and the Greek, Latin, medieval and modern—whom they so deeply influenced. There is, too, the Hindu, Buddhist and Christian teaching expressed in such great monuments as the Indian temples, Barabudur (the Chartres of Asia) and Ajanta, Chartres itself and the Sistine Chapel.

Finally, there are the mystics of feeling, and the mystical philosophers. In God-loving India the poets, musicians, sculptors and painters inspired by the spiritual worship of Krishna and Rama, as well as the philosophic mystics from the Upanishads onward. The two great Taoists Lao-tze and Chuang-tze and the Sung mystical painters in China, Rumi and other sufis in Islam, Plato and Plotinus, followed by 'Dionysius', Eckhart, St. John of the Cross and (in our view) Dante and other great mystics and mystical painters in many Christian lands.

Mankind is hungry, but the feast is there, though it is locked up and hidden away. It is the aim of this Series to put it within reach, so that, like the heroes of Homer, we may stretch forth our hands to the good cheer laid before us.

No doubt the great religions differ in fundamental respects. But they are not nearly so far from one another as they seem. We think they are further off than they are largely because we so often misunderstand and misrepresent them. Those whose own religion is dogmatic have often been as ready to learn from other teachings as those who are liberals in religion. Above all, there is an enormous amount of common ground in the great religions, concerning, too, the most fundamental matters. There is frequent agreement on the Divine Nature; God is the One, Self-subsisting Reality, knowing Himself, and therefore loving and rejoicing in Himself. Nature and finite spirits are in some way subordinate kinds of Being, or merely appearances of the Divine, the One. The three stages of the way of man's approach or return to God are in essence the same in Christian and non-Christian teaching: an ethical stage, then one of knowledge and love, leading to the mystical union of the soul with God. Each stage will be illustrated in these volumes.

Something of all this may (it is hoped) be learnt from the books and pictures in this Series. Read and pondered with a desire to learn, they will help men and women to find 'fulness of life', and peoples to live together in greater understanding and harmony. To-day the earth is beautiful, but men are disillusioned and afraid. But there may come a day, perhaps not a distant day, when there will be a renaissance of man's spirit: when men will be innocent and happy amid the beauty of the world, or their eyes will be opened to see that egoism and strife are folly, that the universe is fundamentally spiritual, and that men are the sons of God.

> They shall not hurt nor destroy
> In all My holy mountain:
> For all the earth shall be full of the
>   knowledge of the Lord
> As the waters cover the sea.
>
> THE EDITORS

PREFACE

Within the limits of this little book are brought together from the sacred scriptures of Buddhism, Islam and Christianity selected passages which reflect the belief that the Founder of the religion was not simply a human being but was possessed of supernatural qualities and characteristics.

Because of the need for brevity the book takes it for granted that Gautama, Muhammad and Jesus did exist as human teachers and that their personalities and teaching provided in each case the impetus for the development of fresh religious experiences and ideas which in time gave rise to the three great religions which we know today. There is a sufficient weight of scholarship which supports this view in each case and fully justifies the assumption. This will be seen to imply a somewhat different point of view from that adopted, for example, by Dr. Conze who, in his recent book on Buddhism prefers to believe that the existence of Gautama as an individual is a matter of little importance.[1] This may be the case for those who wish to study Buddhism only from the standpoint of its ultimate development but to the student of the history of religions the existence of the Founder and the possibility of knowing his original gospel must remain matters of continual interest and importance. For the particular study with which this book deals they will be seen to be of considerable significance.

The need for brevity has also largely dictated the form in which the material is presented. The sacred

[1] E. Conze. *Buddhism. Its Essence and Development.* Oxf. 1951. See esp. pp. 27-28 and 34.

writings are allowed to tell their own story and comments have been restricted to those which are required either to make clear the meaning of the texts or to summarise the main conclusions of scholars who have considered at some length some of the problems which the texts themselves raise.

The transliteration of proper names and of theological terms has been standardised in each case as far as possible but where quotations of translations are given the translator's own form of transliteration has generally been retained.

I am indebted to my friend Dr. Alan Phillips both for assistance in the reading of proofs and also for valuable criticisms and suggestions. My wife's help in the preparation of the Index has greatly facilitated this task.

F.H.H.

CONTENTS

GENERAL INTRODUCTION	page 5
PREFACE	9

THE BUDDHA

1	The Sources	15
2	The Birth of the Buddha	20
3	The Call	31
4	The Ministry	40
5	His Death	47
6	His Supernatural Character	53
7	Buddhology of the Mahāyāna	63

THE PROPHET

8	The Sources	71
9	The Pre-Existence and Birth of the Prophet	76
10	The Call	85
11	The Ministry	92
12	The Death of the Prophet and His Heavenly Intercession	106
13	The Apotheosis of the Prophet	115

THE CHRIST

14	The Sources	121
15	The Pre-Existence, Conception and Birth of the Christ	125
16	The Call	134
17	The Ministry	138
18	The Death, Resurrection and Ascension of the Christ	146
19	The Christ	151
20	Some Reflections	156
INDEX		167

THE BUDDHA

ONE

THE SOURCES

Our sources for a study of the Buddha fall into two main groups—the sacred writings of the Hīnayāna, or the 'Lesser Vehicle', and those of the Mahāyāna or the 'Greater Vehicle'. The Hīnayāna tradition reflects that interpretation of Buddhism which centres attention on the historical Gautama in much the same way as the Gospels do upon Christ, and has been more or less preserved in Ceylon and Burma. The Mahāyāna is Buddhism as it has developed in countries like China and Japan and which interprets the historical Buddha (called here Sākyamuni) as a manifestation of the Absolute.

(a) *The Sacred Scriptures of the Hīnayāna.*

Pāli is the language of the canon of the Hīnayāna: it seems to have been a 'translation' language, in much the same way as the Greek of the New Testament is a translation of the Aramaic which would have been the actual language spoken by Jesus. For Gautama taught in the Kingdoms of Kosala and Magadha in northern India and would no doubt have used the dialects of those states.

The Pāli of the Buddhist canon seems, moreover, to have been an artificial literary language of which the origin is not certainly known. It is plain that it was not in use until after the time of the famous Indian Emperor Asoka—the zealous apostle of the Hīnayāna who reigned during the 3rd century B.C. Asoka left behind him a number of Edicts—inscriptions carved in rocks and pillars, which consist largely of injunctions to righteous and fraternal conduct and refer to passages contained in the Pāli literature. The language of the Asokan rock inscriptions is closely akin to that of the Pāli documents which have come down to us, but it seems to be of a less highly polished character and is therefore probably earlier in date, so that in all probability the Pāli literature as we now know it was not put together until some time after the 3rd century B.C.

However, the fact that certain passages from the Pāli books are referred to in the Asokan inscriptions suggests the existence in the 3rd century B.C. either of an oral tradition, or of written records earlier than our present Pāli sources, or of both. That a fairly extensive oral tradition was in existence is likely when we remember that it was the habit of Indian teachers to encourage their disciples to commit to memory the essential parts of their doctrine. Indeed Gautama himself would seem to have adopted this practice, for he is reported to have said to his hearers on one occasion, 'This is the precise meaning, which you should treasure up in your memories accordingly'.[1] That the Eastern mind was trained to be retentive and most reliable is generally agreed, and this fact alone makes it likely that a considerable part of the original teaching of Gautama was handed on faithfully until it was written down. The art of writing was certainly known in India in the 6th and 5th centuries B.C., but was very little practised for the writing of books, and the probability is that the teaching of Gautama was not committed to writing at once but circulated in oral form for some time after his death.

The actual date of the Pāli canon as we know it today is still a matter of discussion among scholars. Orthodox Buddhist tradition, handed down in the works of the famous Singhalese commentator Buddhaghosa (5th

[1] *Majj. Nik.* III, 199. *S.B.B.* Vol. VI, p. 266.

century A.D.), is naturally anxious to date the compilation of its sacred documents as early as possible. It says that immediately after Gautama's death a great Council of five hundred monks met at Rājagaha about 477 B.C., and that the authorised version of the sayings of the Master as set forth in the Vinaya and the Dhamma (the Sutta Pitaka) and as rehearsed by Upāli and Ānanda, two of the most famous of the early followers of Gautama, was established and fixed. It asserts that this first Council was followed by three more; at Vesālt a hundred years later, called the Great Council (Mahāsangiti), at which questions of monastic discipline were settled and the Vinaya and Dhamma again rehearsed; at Pātaliputta under the patronage of King Asoka, at about 247 B.C., to eliminate schisms; and at Kanishka, about A.D. 100, about which no details are given. It is not clear how far this tradition of the four Buddhist General Councils may be accepted at its face value: some scholars indeed would go so far as to say that the first three Councils are but names without historical reality. It is, however, quite feasible that on the death of the Buddha his chief disciples would have gathered in council and tried to make a summary of his teaching, relying upon the memories of one or two of his most intimate followers. Later Councils would no doubt be called in order to deal with corruptions and heresies and to try to free the original tradition from later accretions. Thus there is nothing inherently improbable in the idea of a number of such Councils, though the orthodox tradition about them may be unreliable in some of its details.

Probably the most recent and authoritative work dealing with this subject is Dr. B. C. Law's *A History of Pāli Literature*,[1] and he seems quite ready to use the Buddhist tradition of the Councils as historical landmarks

[1] London, 1933.

in the development of the Pāli canon. His chief conclusions are as follows:

(1) The 1st century A.D. 'Milinda Pañha', which refers to Pāli books or some chapters of them by name, contains evidence that the division of the canon into three Pitakas and five Nikāyas was well established by that time.

(2) The canon became finally closed some time before the beginning of the Christian era, and so we can safely fix the last quarter of the 1st century B.C. as the 'terminus ad quem'.

(3) The Dīgha Nikāya is to be assigned to a pre-Asokan date.
 The Majjhima Nikāya to a period not more than a hundred years after Buddha's death.
 The Samyutta Nikāya to a period 'not far beyond Buddha's death'.
 The Anguttara Nikāya to the same period as the Majjhima, and the Khuddaka Nikāya to the period following that which saw the formation of the first four Nikāyas.

Among the sections of the Pāli canonical literature which will be particularly referred to are the following:

(a) The Dīgha, Majjhima and Samyutta Nikāyas, containing accounts of the discourses of the Buddha.

(b) The Khuddaka Nikāya, especially the Sutta Nipāta and the Jātaka Tales.

All these books form part of the second of the three Pitakas known as the Sutta or Discourse 'Basket'.

Besides the existence of the Pāli literature, there are extant some portions of Sanskrit translations, as well as translations into Chinese and Tibetan, made either from

Sanskrit or from Pāli, all of which also partially reflect the Hīnayāna point of view.

(b) *The Sacred Scriptures of the Mahāyāna.*
Mahāyāna doctrine was first expounded by Nargajuna in the 2nd century A.D. and it is probable that some of the Mahāyāna sutras were in existence a century, or even two centuries earlier, but it is impossible to point to any one of them as belonging certainly to the 1st century A.D.

They exist now as a whole in Chinese and Tibetan translations. In form they are a continuation of the same type of literature as that of the Hīnayāna—discourses purporting to have been delivered by Buddha at various places, usually during his earthly career. But they are expressly termed Mahāyāna sutras and frequently disagree with the doctrine contained in the older collections.

The canonical texts of the different Mahāyāna sects and schools are too numerous to mention here. The reader is referred to the details given in such books as Mrs. Suzuki's *Mahāyāna Buddhism*, Chapter 5[1] and to M. Steinilber-Oberlin's *Buddhist Sects of Japan*, pp. 268 ff.[2] For translations into English of both Hīnayāna and Mahāyāna texts, reference may be made to the series *Sacred Books of the East*, edited by Max Muller and published by the Oxford University Press. Some Pāli texts have also been translated in the series *Sacred Books of the Buddhists*, also published by the Oxford University Press,[3] and others in the editions of the Pāli Text Society.[4]

[1] Published by The Buddhist Lodge, London, 1938.
[2] George Allen and Unwin, 1938.
[3] These include the Jātaka Stories, the Dīgha and the Majjhima Nikāyas.
[4] *Sacred Books of the East* are here referred to as *S.B.E.*, *Sacred Books of the Buddhists* as *S.B.B.*

TWO

THE BIRTH OF THE BUDDHA

The birth of Gautama Buddha is usually thought to have taken place about the year 560 B.C., at Kapilavatthu (or Kapilavastu) in Northern India, on the borders of Nepal. Buddha is said to have chosen king Suddhodana for his father, and queen Mahāmāyā, Māyā the great, as his mother. According to Buddhist belief Gautama had suffered many births and rebirths before he was eventually born of Māyā in his last existence. Having in a previous existence made the resolution to become a Buddha, he eventually came to birth in the 'Tusita heaven' where he stayed until the time came for his last existence.[1] Then he chose the time, the continent, the country, his father and his mother, and taking leave of the gods, descended to earth.[2] References to this pre-existence and final birth are scattered about in the Canon.

'For a long time have I known, monks, the wished-for, desired, dear, delightful and severally enjoyed results of

---

[1] The Tusita heaven was regarded as the fourth of the six heavens of the world of desire. Buddhists thought of the whole of existence, from the lowest hell to the limit of existence, as made up of the three worlds of desire, form and formlessness. It is not possible to identify the formless world (the 'arupa dhatu') with the Western Christian 'Heaven'. In fact Buddhists regarded existence in any of these worlds as having in some sense the nature of evil, because 'nirvāna', the true goal, could not be thought of as existence in any positive sense. (McGovern, *A Manual of Buddhist Philosophy*; Vol. I pp. 60-70. Lond. 1923.)

[2] A continuous account of the Buddha's decision to enter the last existence is first found in the Jātaka Commentary, which Thomas reckons to be a translation of an older Pāli work. *The Life of Buddha*, 2nd Ed., Lond. 1931, p. 274. The Jātaka itself, containing verses belonging to 551 tales of previous existences of Buddha, is part of the Khuddaka-Nikāya of the Pāli Canon. See on this Dr. Malalasekera's *Pāli literature of Ceylon*, p. 117 ff. London 1928.

good works done for a long time. Having practised benevolence for seven years, I did not return to this world during seven aeons of consummation and restoration. Yea, monks, at the consummation of an aeon I was an Angel of Splendour, and at the restoration I rose again in the empty palace of the Brahmas. Yea, then, O monks, I was a Brahma—the Great Brahmā, conquering, unconquered, all-seeing, controlling. And thirty six times O monks, was I Sakko, the lord of the angels; many hundreds of times I was a king, a righteous emperor, a king of righteousness (or, king by right, the Epic title of a Hindu suzerain), victorious in the four quarters, securely established in my country and possessed of the seven treasures. Now what was the doctrine of that religion and kingdom? This is what I thought of it O monks: "What deed of mine is this the fruit of? Of what deed is this the result, whereby now I am thus magical and mighty?" This is what I thought of it O monks: "This is the fruit of three deeds of mine, of three deeds the result, whereby now I am thus magical and mighty, to wit: alms, control and abstinence".' (Itivutt. 22). 'Mindful and conscious the Bodhisatta stayed in the Tusita body. Throughout his full span of life, the Bodhisatta stayed in the Tusita body. Mindful and conscious the Bodhisatta descending from the Tusita body entered the womb of his mother.' (Majj. Nik. III. 119.)

It has to be remembered that Buddhism took its rise in India and inherited from Hinduism[1] the view that human life may be but one of a whole series of existences, from the lowest forms of animal and insect life to that of the gods of the celestial worlds. Beings can and do pass through some or all of these forms of existence as a result

[1] The term 'Hinduism' is understood to include 'Brahmanism', as in Conze, op. cit. p. 34.

of a series of rebirths, the shape of which is decided by their 'Karma' or 'deeds' in previous lives. This is the doctrine of 'Saṃsāra' which in the form adopted by the early Buddhists involved not the rebirth of a soul or 'attā' (Sanskrit: 'ātman') but simply the inevitable 'dying out' and 'rekindling' of the flame of existence. It could be brought to an end according to Gautama's teaching, by man's becoming 'enlightened'—the aim with which a Buddhist became a member of the Order, followed the Buddha and took the 'middle Path' between asceticism and indulgence.[1]

Now as we have seen, the canonical writings assert that Gautama (referred to as the 'bodhisattva' or 'Buddha-to-be') had, in common with all men, passed through the usual cycle of existences. In this sense therefore, there was nothing about Gautama's pre-existence which set him apart from other men. Yet it has to be noticed that only of Gautama and of other distinguished Bodhisattvas is the history of their previous lives—or something like it—brought before our eyes. There can be no doubt that the canonical writings mean us to pay particular attention to their pre-existence, and to that of the Buddha in particular, as being vitally important for the full appreciation of the significance of the final birth in which Gautama appeared on earth as the enlightened Saviour of men. We are not allowed to imagine that this birth, so vitally important for the welfare of the human race, had such ordinary antecedents that it can be passed over in silence. If for all men some degree of pre-existence was, in Buddhist eyes, true, yet it is true that of this One above all it was not only true but so important that it must be especially noticed and remembered.

[1] The disciple who had reached this goal was called 'Arahant' or 'Worthy'.

This same truth is also emphasised by the canonical accounts of the supernatural conception and birth of the Buddha. Thus the Majj. Nik. declares that when Buddha entered the womb of Māyā the celestial worlds were stirred:

'When the Bodhisatta, descending from the Tusita body, entered the womb of his mother, then in the world with its gods, Māras, and Brahmas, among the creatures with ascetics, brahmins, gods and men, appears a boundless great splendour surpassing the divine majesty of the gods. And in the spaces between the worlds, gloomy, open, dark, of darkness and obscurity, where too this moon and sun so mighty and majestic are unable to shine, even there a boundless great splendour appears surpassing the divine majesty of the gods. And the beings that have been reborn there perceive one another by that splendour and think, "Surely sirs, there are other beings that have been reborn here." And this universe of ten thousand worlds shakes and trembles and quakes, and a boundless great splendour appears in the world surpassing the divine majesty of the gods.' (Majj. III, 120.)

Divine protection is given to his mother:

'When the Bodhisatta has entered his mother, four gods approach her to protect the four quarters (saying) "Let nought human or superhuman or anything else hurt the Bodhisatta or the Bodhisatta's mother."'

No mention is made of the father in connection with his birth: his mother is said to have separated herself from the things of the world and to have brought forth the child in an unusual manner:

' When the Bodhisatta has entered his mother, the Bodhisatta's mother has the regular moral qualities of abstaining from taking life, from theft, from wrongful indulgence in sensual desires, from falsehood, and from the occasions of carelessness in the use of intoxicants.

'When the Bodhisatta has entered his mother, there arises in the Bodhisatta's mother no thought of men connected with the senses, and the Bodhisatta's mother is not to be overcome by any man of passionate heart.

'When the Bodhisatta has entered his mother, the Bodhisatta's mother is in possession of the five senses, and is surrounded and endowed with the five senses.

'When the Bodhisatta has entered his mother, no sickness arises in the Bodhisatta's mother, she is happy with unwearied body.

'And the Bodhisatta's mother sees within her body the Bodhisatta with all his limbs and complete sense-organs. Like a beryl jewel, pure, noble, eight-sided, excellently worked, and threaded with a blue, yellow, red, white, or yellowish thread: a man who could see might take it in his hand and looking at it say, "this beryl jewel, pure, noble, eight-sided, excellently worked, is threaded with blue, yellow," etc. etc. Even so the Bodhisatta.

'When the Bodhisatta has been born seven days, the Bodhisatta's mother dies. She is reborn in a Tusita body.

'As other women give birth nine or ten months (lunar) after conception, not so does the Bodhisatta's mother give birth. The Bodhisatta's mother gives birth to the Bodhisatta ten months after conception. As other women give birth sitting or lying down, not so does the Bodhisatta's mother give birth. The Bodhisatta's mother gives birth to the Bodhisatta standing.

'When the Bodhisatta is born, first the gods take him, and then human beings.

'When the Bodhisatta is born, he does not fall to the ground. Four gods take him and set him before his mother, saying, "Rejoice lady, A mighty son has been born to thee."

'When the Bodhisatta is born, he is born clean, unstained with liquid, unstained with phlegm, unstained with blood, unstained with any filth, but pure and clean. Just as when a gem is placed on Benares cloth, the gem does not stain the cloth, nor the cloth the gem, and why? On account of the pureness of both—even so when the Bodhisatta is born, he is born clean. . . .

'When the Bodhisatta is born, two streams of water fall from the sky, one of cold and one of hot water, wherewith they perform the washing of the Bodhisatta and his mother.

'As soon as born the Bodhisatta firmly standing with even feet goes towards the North with seven long steps, a white parasol being held over him (by the gods). He surveys all the quarters, and in a lordly voice says, "I am the chief in the world, I am the best in the world, I am the first in the world. This is my last birth. There is now no existence again".' (Majj. Nik. III, 120-123.) (cf. Dīgha. Nik. II, 12-15.)

A good deal of discussion has centred around the question whether the birth of Buddha as thus described in the Buddhist canon may rightly be called a 'Virgin Birth'. Dr. E. J. Thomas points out that there is in fact a difference here between the view-point of the older and that of the later accounts. The oldest accounts of Buddha's ancestry appear to pre-suppose nothing abnormal about his birth, and merely speak of his being well-born on his mother's and father's side for seven generations back. (Dīgha. I, 113)

According to later versions he is born not as other human beings, but descends from the Tusita heaven by his own choice and with this his father is not concerned. There can obviously be no question about the fact that the Buddhist canon regards the birth of the Buddha as miraculous, though it is by no means clear that it is regarded as having been a strictly 'Virgin Birth'. Dr. Thomas's conclusion here is that 'This is not properly a Virgin birth, but it may be called "parthogenetic", that is Suddhodana was not his progenitor'.[1]

The Majj. Nik. tells of the appearance of a celestial light which causes gods and angels to consider Buddha's birth:

'Ānanda, when the Bodhisatta leaves his mother's womb, then in the world of the angels, together with those of Māra and Brahmā, and unto the race of philosophers and Brahmins, princes and peoples, there appears a splendour limitless and eminent, transcending the angelic might of the angels; and even in the boundless realms of space, with their darkness upon darkness, where yonder sun and moon, so magical, so mighty, are felt not in the sky, there too appears the splendour limitless and eminent, transcending the very might of the angels, so that beings who are born there consider among themselves by reason of that splendour', etc. etc., as described above in connection with the conception of Buddha. (Majj. III, 123-124)

Of more interest, however, is the story in the Sutta Nipāta of the visit of Asita the hermit to the infant Buddha:

[1] *The Life of Buddha as Legend and History*, p. 36.

Rejoicing, delighted, the hosts of the Thirty,
Sakko the leader and angels white-stoled,
Seizing their robes and chanting high praises,
Did Asita the hermit see in noonday rest.

Seeing the angels with minds gladdened, ecstatic,
He made obeisance and forthwith spake thus:
'Why is the assembly of the angels exceedingly pleased?
Wherefore do you seize your robes and wave them?

'When there was a battle with the devils,
A victory for the angels and devils defeated,
Then there was not such astonishment:
What portent is it that the deities have seen that they rejoice?

'They shout and sing and make music,
They whirl their arms and dance:
I ask you, O dwellers upon Meru's height,
Remove my doubt quickly, O venerable ones!'

      (The Angels answer)

'The Bodhisatta, the best and matchless jewel,
Is born for weal and welfare in the world of men,
In the town of the Sakyas, in the region of Lumbini:
Therefore are we joyful and exceeding glad.

'He, the highest of all beings, the head person,
The chief (lit. bull) of men, the highest of all creatures,
Will set rolling the wheel (of religion) in the hermit-named forest,
Like the roaring mighty lion mastering the deer'.

Hearing that sound, he came down from the Heaven of Content,
And entered Suddhodana's abode:
There seated he addressed the Sakyas thus:
'Where is the prince? (or boy) I desire to see him'.

There was the prince with glowing gold,
Very skilfully wrought in the forge's mouth,
Blazing in glory and the lofty air of beauty:
Unto him named Asita the Sakyas showed their son.

Seeing the prince aglow like flame,
Pure as the chief of stars wandering in the sky,
Like the burning sun in autumn free from clouds,
He joyfully obtained great delight.

The angels held in air a canopy,
Many-branched and thousand-ringed:
Chowries with golden staves were fanned;
Unseen were they who carried the chowries and the
 canopy.

The hermit with matted hair, called Kanhasiri,
When he saw the yellow trappings bright as a golden
 piece,
And the white canopy held over his head,
Received him delighted and happy.

But when he had received the chief of the Sakyas,
He who was wishing for him, and knew the signs and
 the Hymns
With placed thoughts gave utterance to the speech:
'This is the unrivalled one, the highest among bipeds'.

Then, remembering his own migration,
He was saddened and shed tears.
Seeing this, the Sakyas asked the weeping hermit
Whether there were danger for the Prince.

Seeing the Sakyas sad, the hermit spake:
'I remember naught unhappy for the Prince:
There will be no danger at all for him;
He is no ordinary being. Be not dismayed.

'The Prince will reach the summit of perfect enlightenment:

Seeing supernatural purity, he will set rolling the
wheel of the Doctrine,
Out of pity, for the weal of the multitude,
And his religion will be prosperous.

'My life below will not be long,
And in the midst of it all my appointed time will
come:
I shall not hear the Doctrine of the peerless leader;
Therefore am I afflicted, unfortunate, and suffering'.[1]

A version which is possibly older than the one quoted above is given in the Nidāna-kathā, the introductory part of the commentary of the Jātaka in the Khuddaka-Nikāya. In this account there is no sage (Skt. rishi) but a 'tāpasa' or ascetic; his name moreover is not Asita but Kāladevala, or 'Devala the black', and he is not a stranger to the king, but gets his living by haunting the palace. On seeing the boy he smiles and then weeps. This incident of smiling and weeping is a very common Indian folk tale feature, indicating that this particular version, which claims to be a translation from the Singhalese, bears clear marks of its source.

The story of the 'Buddhist Simeon' has, of course, been compared with the New Testament story of the reception of the infant Christ in the Temple, told in St. Matthew ii. 25 ff.; it also has obvious affinities with the Lukan story of the appearance of the angels to the shepherds. Certain scholars indeed, have argued that the Buddhist legend is the original of the Christian story.[2] Dr. Kennedy seems to assume that the Sutta Nipāta is largely a compilation of the Christian era, which would rule out dependence of the Christian upon the Buddhist sources.

[1] *S.B.E.*, Vol. X, Part 2, pp. 124 ff. The version quoted here is that of Edmunds: *Buddhist and Christian Gospels;* revised by M. Anesaki. Philadelphia, 1914.
[2] See Thomas, *Life of the Buddha*, p. 43.

But Dr. B. C. Law has shown that the evidence available suggests that the whole of the Khuddaka Nikāya, including both the Sutta Nipāta and the Jātaka Book, was already a part of the closed Pāli canon before the end of the 1st century B.C.[1] The possibility of the influence of the Buddhist legend on the Christian must therefore at any rate be kept open.

The problem of whether or not there is any connection between the Buddhist and Christian stories is however inevitably bound up with the much larger question of the relations, if any, between Buddhist and Christian communities in the first century A.D. and this will be discussed later. For the moment it seems sufficient to point out that in this case there are noticeable differences between the Buddhist and Christian legends. Asita was not expecting a Buddha; he did not depart in peace, but with lamentation; and he did not live to see the Buddha come.

A more important consideration however, than any actual connection of an historical kind between the two stories is the fact that the Buddhist canon contains versions of a legend, the purpose of which is again plainly to emphasise the supreme importance of the appearance on earth of the Buddha. As the story of the super-normal birth in the Buddhist tradition is designed to set the Buddha apart from ordinary mortals, so here too the great significance of the birth is attested by the attentions and the prophecies of the holy man:

> 'Seeing the Sakyas sad, the hermit spake:
> "I remember naught unhappy for the Prince:
> There will be no danger at all for him;
> He is no ordinary being. Be not dismayed".'

[1] Dr. Kennedy's Article on the Buddhist 'Gospels of the Infancy', in *J.R.A.S.*, 1917.
Law: *A History of Pāli Literature*, London, 1933.
Cf. Edmunds, *Buddhist and Christian Gospels*, Vol. I, pp. 85-87, Introduction.

THREE

THE CALL

The sacred writings reveal comparatively little interest in that part of the Buddha's life which preceded his call and his appearance as a great Teacher.

Various accounts are given of the way in which he attained to his first trance, of which the following from the Majj. Nik. seems to have been the basis:

'Then I thought,' Buddha says, 'now I realise that when my father the Sakyan was working, I was seated under the cool shade of a rose-apple tree, and without sensual desires, without evil ideas, I attained and abode in the first trance of joy and pleasure arising from seclusion, and combined with reasoning and investigation. Perhaps this is the way to enlightenment.'[1]

An interesting addition to these stories is found in the Lalita-vistara, a Sanskrit account of the life of the Buddha from his decision to be born down to his first sermon: it is the legend of the visit of the Buddha-to-be to the writing school. He is taken in great pomp, and the writing master Viśvāmitra falls on the ground before his glory. The boy takes the writing tablet, asks which alphabet his master is going to teach him, and gives a list of 64 kinds, including those of the Chinese and the Huns. When the boys repeat the alphabet, at each letter a moral truth is uttered, which begins with, or contains that letter, and this takes place through the wonderful power of the Buddha-to-be.

Only one other reference to this early period is given

[1] I. 246.

in the Canon—Buddha's account of his luxurious life as a prince:

'I was delicate, O Monks, extremely delicate, excessively delicate. In my father's dwelling lotus-pools had been made, in one blue lotuses, in another red, in another white, all for my sake. I used no sandal-wood that was not of Benares, my dress was of Benares cloth, my tunic, my under-robe and cloak. Night and day a white parasol was held over me so that I should not be touched by cold or heat, by dust or weeds or dew. I had three palaces, one for the cold season, one for the hot, and one for the season of rains. Through the four rainy months I did not come down from the palace; and as in the dwellings of others food from the husks of rice is given to the slaves and workmen together with sour gruel, so in my father's dwelling rice and meat was given to the slaves and workmen.'

(Augutt. I, 145; cf. Majj. I, 504.)

Evidently the Buddha was married as a young prince, though there seems considerable disagreement between the sacred writers as to the name of his wife: She is known variably as Bhaddakaccā, Yasodharā, and Subhaddakā; she is also called 'Bimbā the beautiful'. All the accounts seem to agree however that by her Buddha had a son, whose name was Rāhula. The Dīgha Nikāya implies that the Buddha left the world at the age of twenty-nine, and died at the age of eighty. (II, 151.)

When we come to the story of Buddha's call, or renunciation of the world, the canonical accounts become much fuller:

'Then, O monks, did I, endowed with such majesty and such excessive delicacy, think this, "An ignorant, ordinary person who is himself subject to old age, not beyond the sphere of old age, on seeing an old man is troubled, ashamed, and disgusted, extending the thought to himself. I too am subject to old age, not beyond the sphere of old age, and should I, who am subject to old age, not beyond the sphere of old age, on seeing an old man be troubled, ashamed, and disgusted?" This seemed to me not fitting. As I thus reflected on it, all the elation (lit: 'mada' or 'intoxication') in youth utterly disappeared.'

The same formula is then repeated of sickness and death and it is said, 'the elation in life utterly disappeared'.

(Ang. I, 145 ff.; Cf. Majj. I, 504.)

A still more general description is found in Majj. I, 163.

'Thus, O monks, before my enlightenment, while yet a Bodhisatta and not fully enlightened, being myself subject to birth, I sought out the nature of old age, of sickness, of death, of sorrow, of impurity. Then I thought, "what if I being myself subject to birth were to seek out the nature of birth . . . and having seen the wretchedness of the nature of birth, were to seek out the unborn, the supreme peace of Nirvāna".'

Of the long, extra-canonical accounts of Buddha's flight from home the canon refers only to one incident. In the Khuddaka-Nikāya the elder Moggallāna visits the heaven of the Thirty-three and sees the god Kanthaka, who explains that he was formerly Buddha's horse and tells the story of the flight. (Vimānavatthu VII. 7, *S.B.B.* Vol. 12, pp. 115-117).

The Majj. Nik. also preserves a version of the Renunciation which makes Buddha leave home when still a boy:

'Now before my enlightenment, while yet a Bodhisatta

and not yet fully enlightened, I thought, oppressive is life in a house, a place of dust. In the free air is abandonment of the world. Not easy is it for him who dwells in a house to practice a completely full, completely pure, and perfect religious life. What if I remove my hair and beard, and putting on yellow robes go forth from a house to a houseless life.

'Now at another time, while yet a boy, a black-haired lad in the prime of youth, in the first stage of life, while my unwilling mother and father wept with tear-stained faces, I cut off my hair and beard, and putting on yellow robes went forth from a house to a houseless life.' (I.240.)

After his retirement from the world Buddha practises severe austerities in order to find enlightenment and peace: a long account of his experiences is given in the Majj. Nik. of which the conclusion may be quoted:

'Thus with mind concentrated, purified, cleansed, with the defilements gone, supple, dexterous, firm, and impassible, I directed my mind to the knowledge of the destruction of the āsavas.[1] I duly realised (the truth) "this is pain", I duly realised (the truth) "this is the cause of pain", I duly realised (the truth) "this is the destruction of pain", and I duly realised (the truth) "this is the way that leads to the destruction of pain". I duly realised "these are the āsavas" ... "this is the cause of the āsavas" ... "this is the destruction of the āsavas" ... "this is the way that leads to the destruction of the āsavas". As I thus knew and thus perceived, my mind was emancipated from the āsavas of sensual desire, from the āsavas of desire for existence, and from the āsava of ignorance. And in me emancipated arose the knowledge

[1] 'Intoxicants' or 'defilements', which tie the mind down to individual existence.

of my emancipation. I realised that destroyed is rebirth, the religious life has been led, done is what was to be done, there is nought (for me) beyond this world. This was the third knowledge that I gained in the last watch of the night. Ignorance was dispelled, knowledge arose. Darkness was dispelled, light arose. So is it with him who abides vigilant, strenuous, and resolute.'
(Majj. I. 21 ff.)

During this time and immediately after his enlightenment Buddha is tempted by Māra the evil one:

(a) While he is engaged in the Great Struggle Māra with his nine hosts tempts him to abandon the struggle:

'To me intent on striving by the Neranjara river, exerting myself in contemplation to win the calm of peace, came Namuci (the name of a Vedic demon applied to Māra) uttering compassionate speech.

' "Lean thou art and ill-favoured, near to thee is death. Death hath a thousand parts, only one part of thee is life. Live, good sir: life is better. Living thou shalt do good works.

' "If thou livest the religious life, if thou sacrificest the fire-sacrifice, much good is stored up. What hast thou to do with striving?

' "Hard is the path of striving, hard to perform, and hard to attain."

'These verses did Māra speak, standing in the presence of the Buddha.

' Then to Māra speaking thus did the Lord say: "Friend of the slothful, evil one, for thine own sake hast thou come hither.

"No need for even the least work of merit is found in me. Them that have need of merits let Māra deign to address.

"Faith is found in me, and heroism and wisdom. Why dost thou ask about life from me, who am thus intent?

"The streams even of rivers may this wind dry up. How should not my blood dry up, when I am intent?

"When the blood dries up, the bile and phlegm dry up. When the flesh wastes away, still more does the mind become tranquil. Still more does my mindfulness, my wisdom and concentration become firm.

"While I live thus, having attained the last sensation, my mind looks not to lusts. Behold the purity of a being.

"Lusts (kāmā) are thy first army, the second is called Aversion (arati). Thy third is Hunger-and-thirst. The fourth is called Craving (tanhā).

"Thy fifth Sloth-and-indolence, thy sixth is called Cowardice. Thy seventh is Doubt, thy eighth Hypocrisy and Stupidity.

"Gain, Fame, Honour, and Glory falsely obtained, the Lauding of oneself and Condemning of others.

"This Namuci, is thy army, the host of thee the Black One. The coward overcomes it not, but he that overcomes it gains happiness.

"I am wearing munja-grass (a sign that the warrior intends to devote himself in battle); shame on life in this world! Better to me is death in battle than that I should live defeated.

"Plunged in this battle some ascetics and brahmins are (not) found. They know not the way on which the virtuous go.

"Seeing the army on all sides I go to meet Māra arrayed with his elephant in the battle. He shall not drive me from my post.

"That army of thine, which the world of gods and men

conquers not, even that with my wisdom will I smite, as an unbakened earthen bowl with a stone.

"Having controlled my intention and well-set mindfulness from kingdom to kingdom will I wander, training disciples far and wide.

"Not careless they, but intent, and performing the teaching of me who am free from lust, they shall go where having gone they do not grieve."'

'(Māra speaks) "For seven years have I followed the Lord step by step. I can find no entrance to the All-enlightened, the watchful one.

' "As a crow went after a stone that looked like a lump of fat, thinking, surely here I shall find a tender morsel, here perchance is something sweet,

' "And finding no sweetness there, the crow departed thence, so like a crow attacking a rock, in disgust, I leave Gotama."

'The lute of Māra who was overcome with grief slipped from beneath his arm. Then in dejection the Yakkha disappeared from thence.' (Sutta Nipāta 425-449; *S.B.E.* XII. pp. 69 ff. This translation is from Thomas op. cit. pp. 72-73.)

Other references to the Temptations are:

(b) In Samy. I. IV. 3, 5 and Sutta Nipāta 835 it is said that in the fifth week before his Enlightenment Buddha was tempted by three daughters of Māra.

(c) After his Enlightenment Buddha was assailed by doubt. (Vinaya Mahavagga I. 5; Dīgha. II. 35-40; Majj. I. 167-169.)

(d) He was tempted to accomplish his decease and leave men to their fate. (Dīgha. II. 112-114.)

(e) While resting in a forest hut in the Himalayas he was tempted by Māra to exercise his sovereignty and turn the Himalayas into gold. (Samy. I. IV. 2, 10.)

A good deal of attention has been given to the apparent resemblance between the Buddhist account of the Temptation of Buddha by Māra and the Gospel story of Christ's Temptation by Satan; some scholars indeed have sought to show that the Evangelists made use of the Buddhist accounts. Thomas for instance, allows himself to declare: 'It is still possible to maintain that some form of the Buddhist legend was known to the Evangelists, but not by asserting that the scattered events as we know them fit into the legend.' It must be emphasised again however that this problem of a possible literary connection between the various accounts is, for our present purpose, less significant than the fact that the Buddhist scriptures regard it as important to stress the truth that the call of the Buddha and the initiation of his sacred ministry cannot be fully understood merely in their temporal setting. The accounts of the renunciation and the temptation are framed in such a way as to emphasise their supernatural significance.

No doubt it is true that the long accounts of Buddha's austerities are of the nature of psychological discourses, the main purpose of which is to make clear to the disciples the right and the wrong way of setting about the attainment of enlightenment. But it seems evident that they also aim at setting forth the Buddha as the enlightened one 'par excellence', who had become the guide and teacher of men, a 'shower of the way' (maggakkhāyin), in whom his followers could have faith.

The verses of the Theras and the Therīs—the monks and nuns of early Buddhism—well illustrate something of this attitude to Buddha:

> 'Past-master he in sooth to guide,
> Into the way of blest security.'
> (Theragāthā 69.)

'All glory to the Exalted One,
Our splendid Lord, the Sākiyas' son!
For he the topmost height hath won,
And dhamma as supreme hath shown.'
(Theragāthā 94; both are quoted in translation from Horner: *Early Buddhist Theory of Man Perfected*, p. 144, Lond. 1936.)

FOUR

THE MINISTRY

Stories of miracles in the Buddhist canon abound, nor are they limited to the Buddha, but are recognised as being a part of the powers of his followers. In the Anguttara Nikāya Buddha is reported as having a discussion with a Brahmin about his miraculous powers:

' "As to the miracle of psychical power ... this kind of miracle Gotamo, appears to me a natural accompaniment of religion. And I think the same of the second, the miracle of mind-reading. But that last one, O Gotamo, that miracle of education, appears to me the most excellent and most refined. Wonderful, O Gotamo, marvellous, O Gotamo, is this good saying of yours; and we hold that you are endowed with all three of these miracles. Gotamo can indeed practise every one of the aforesaid psychical powers...."

'(Buddha replies)

"It is true O Brahmin, that I have attained to all that you have said, and I will furthermore assert that I can do each of the three miracles in question."

'(The Brahmin)

' "But is there, O Gotamo, a single other monk who is endowed with these miracles besides yourself?"

'(The Buddha)

' "Brahmin, not only one, nor a hundred, not two, three,

four or five hundred, but even more monks there are who are endowed with these three miracles."

(Angutt. Nik. III. 60.)

On more than one occasion however, the Buddha is said to have forbidden his followers to perform miracles. According to the story in the Cullavagga, for example, he forbade a repetition of the miracle performed by the elder Pindola at Rājagaha, by which he had risen in the air by magic power (iddhi) and brought down a sandalwood bowl from the end of a long bamboo.

This ban so delighted the heretics present, that the Buddha felt obliged, four months later, to perform a miracle himself. The king's gardener at Sāvatthī was told to sow a seed from a ripe mango, and no sooner had Buddha washed his hands over it than it sprang up into a tree fifty hands high. It would seem that Buddha disapproved of his followers performing miracles in the presence of any but monks:

'Ye are not, O monks, to display psychical power or miracles of super-human kind before the laity. Whoever does so is guilty of a misdemeanour.'[1]

Presumably the ban applied even more to the performance of miracles before unbelievers.

Buddha himself seems not to have hesitated to resort to miracles in order to provide evidence of his character and authority. The most celebrated of these, which he is said to have performed on four separate occasions, is called the 'Miracle of the Pairs' (Yamaka-pātihāriya). Buddha caused himself to rise in the air, flames of fire came from the upper part of his body, and streams of water from the lower part. Then the process was reversed. Next fire came from the right side of his body and water

[1] Cullavagga of Vinaya Pitaka V, 8. *S.B.E.*, Vol. XX, pp. 78-81.

from the left, and so on through twenty-two variations o pairs. He then created a jewelled promenade in the sky, and walking along it, produced the illusion that he was standing, or sitting, or lying down, and varied the illusions in a similar way. On the first occasion of that miracle, Buddha succeeded in converting his father and his court: the Jātaka account says that on the three other occasions that he performed it, it was in order to remove the doubt of the gods, at the meeting with Pātīka—a disciple who was converted by the miracle—and on the occasion of the miracle of the mango-tree recounted above, when the heretics were silenced.[1] This miracle is the subject of an extant 1st-century B.C. carving originating in North-West India.[2]

The Buddhist canon also credits Buddha with nature-miracles and healing-miracles. As examples of the former two may be quoted here:

'Now on that occasion there rained a great unseasonable cloud, and a great flood arose. In the place where the Lord was sojourning, that place was not pervaded by water. Then the Lord reflected, "Suppose now I drive out the water around, and pace in meditation on dust-covered ground in the midst." So the Lord drove out the water around, and paced in meditation upon dust-covered ground in the midst.'[3]

The Jātaka also tells the story of how Buddha brought rain during a period of drought in the kingdom of Kosala:

'Friend Pajjumo, I am distrest for my kinsfolk's sake. I am moral and austere and why sendest thou no rain from heaven? . . . Therewith he called unto Pajjumo, the

---

[1] Thomas 98-99; Note 2. The canonical reference is in Paṭisambhidā-magga I. 125 (of the Khuddaka-Nikāya). (cf. Mahāvastu, III, 115; a Sanskrit work.)
[2] Reproduced in Thomas, facing p. 98.
[3] Mahāvagga of Vinaya Piṭaka, I, 20, 16. S.B.E., XIII, 130-131.

angel-king, as a master might call an attendant or a slave, in this stanza:

> ' "Thunder, O Pajjumo! Destroy the Lord of the crow!
> Deliver the crow unto sorrow, and release me from the same!"

'Even as if ordering an attendant or a slave the future Buddha called to Pajjumo, and delivering a great many folk from the pain of death.'[1]

Of accounts of healing-miracles, the story of the healing of Kassapa at Rājagaha, may be quoted; it is recounted in the Samyutta Nikāya:

'At one season the Lord was staying at Rājagaha... Now at that season S. Kassapo the Great was staying at the Fig-tree Grotto, and was sick, suffering and severely ill. Then the Lord, having arisen from his evening retirement went up to S. Kassapo the Great, and sat on a seat prepared for him ... "Kassapo, there are these seven branches of wisdom thoroughly taught by me, practised and developed; and they conduce to higher knowledge, to full enlightenment, to Nirvana ..." This is what the Lord said, and S. Kassapo the Great was rapt and rejoiced at the utterance of the Lord. And S. Kassapo the Great got up from that sickness; and so his sickness was renounced.'

(Samyutta Nikāya XLVI. II, VI).

A similar account occurs in the same Nikāya of the healing of S. Cunda the Great; in fact the same formula and setting are quoted, which inevitably detract from the historical value of the stories. Nevertheless this need not suggest that some kernel of historical fact may not underlie the narratives.[2]

[1] Jātaka 75.
[2] Samyutta Nikāya XLVI, II, VI.

It is interesting to notice that side by side with stories of the Buddha's healing-miracles the canon also contains accounts of occasions when he did not heal people. Thus we are told that in the eighteenth year he was at Ālavī, where a weaver's daughter, whom the Buddha knew to be 'at the point of death', was converted: unfortunately, on returning home, she was killed by the falling of a part of the loom. The Buddha did not restore her to life, but merely consoled her father with the thought of the frequency of death.[1]

Similarly the monk, Tissa of Sāvatthī was attacked by a malignant disease, and the Buddha, coming to the monastery, heated water to bathe him, in spite of the loathsome nature of the disease, and then washed him and his robes as well, later clothing him in the clean dry garments. After receiving from the Buddha teaching about the body, the monk died and attained Nirvāna.[2] The Buddhist view of life clearly was not such as to make the mere continuation of bodily existence an end to be desired in itself; on the contrary, the supreme end was the attainment of Nirvāna, for which bodily death was one of the preliminary events. Miracles of healing, therefore, would not of themselves always carry with them a *prima facie* conviction of the Buddha's supernatural powers and mission.

Before leaving the subject of the miracles performed by the Buddha, it will be of interest to include a reference to the story, told in the Jātaka, of the lay disciple who walked on the water. This disciple was on his way to Jetavana to see the Buddha:

'He arrived at the bank of the river Aciravatī in the evening. As the ferryman had drawn the boat up on the

---

[1] Dhammapada Commentary, III, 170; translated in *Buddhist Scriptures*, pp. 57-63: trans. E. J. Thomas, London, 1913.
[2] Dhammapada Commentary, I. 319. Thomas, *Life of Buddha*, p. 121.

beach, and had gone to listen to the Doctrine, the disciple saw no boat at the ferry, so finding joy in making Buddha the object of his meditation, he walked across the river. His feet did not sink in the water. He went as though on the surface of the earth, but when he reached the middle he saw waves. Then his joy in meditating on the Buddha grew small, and his feet began to sink. But making firm his joy in meditating on the Buddha he went on the surface of the water, entered Jetavana, saluted the Teacher, and sat on one side.'[1]

The only comment which need be made here is that in India in the pre-Christian era, the idea was commonly held that one of the magic powers to be attained by meditation was that of going over water as if on dry land. The canonical writings frequently refer to Buddha's use of such power.

(b) *The Transfiguration.*
Shortly before the end of his life it is said that on his way to Kusinārā Buddha was presented with a pair of gold-coloured robes by the lay-disciple Pukkusa. The following account of what happened afterwards is taken from the Dīgha Nikāya:

'Now not long after Pukkusa the Mallian had gone S. Ānando placed upon the person of the Lord that pair of gold-cloth robes, burnished and ready to wear. And when so placed upon the person of the Lord it appeared bereft of its brightness.

'And S. Ānando said unto the Lord: "Wonderful, O Lord! Marvellous, O Lord! that the colour of the Tathāgato's skin should be so pure and purified. For when I placed upon the person of the Lord this pair of

[1] Introduction to Jātaka No. 190, quoted Thomas, p. 241.

gold-cloth robes, burnished and ready for wear, it appeared bereft of its brightness."

' "Ānando, it is even so. There are two occasions, Ānando, when the colour of a Tathāgato's skin becomes pure and exceeding purified. What are the two? On the night Ānando, wherein a Tathāgato is supernally enlightened with incomparable and perfect enlightenment, and on the night when he enters Nirvāna with that kind of Nirvāna which leaves no substrata behind: on these two occasions the colour of a Tathāgato's skin becomes pure and exceeding purified. And now, Ānando, this day, in the third watch of the night, in the twin sal-trees, will take place the Tathāgato's passage into Nirvāna. Come Ānando, let us to the river Kakuttha."

' "Even so, Lord," said Ānando, in assent unto the Lord. The pair of burnished gold-cloth robes were brought by Pukkusa:

'The Master, when begirt therewith, in golden colour shone.'

(Dīgha II. 133-134.)

It is worth noticing how this tradition indicates that by means of this 'transfiguration' Ānanda and others may know that Gautama (the Tathāgata) is indeed 'supernally enlightened with incomparable and perfect enlightenment' and will shortly enter 'Nirvāna with that kind of Nirvāna which leaves no substrata behind'. In other words the purpose lying behind the inclusion of the story in the canon is to provide yet further confirmation of Gautama's position as the true enlightened Saviour of men.

FIVE

HIS DEATH

The account of Buddha's last days is contained in three suttas of which the 'Sutta of the Great Decease', the Mahâ Parinibbâna, is the most important.[1] These suttas are a mixture of story and discourse, and they tell the story of Buddha's journey from Rājagaha across the Ganges to Vesālī, and then on to Kusinārā in the country of the Mallas, where he passed away.

There is an interesting story, referred to more than once, of Sāriputta's 'lion roar'. At Nālandā it is said that Sāriputta uttered a 'lion roar' (sīhanāda) of faith in Buddha. 'Such, Lord, is my faith in the Lord, that there has not been, will not be, nor is there now another ascetic or brahmin greater or of more wisdom, that is to say, in enlightenment.' (Dīgha II 81-83. Cf. Dīgha III. 99 ff.) The tendency, here seen at work, to assign to the Buddha a position of unique and supreme importance among holy men, is obviously an indication that at a very early period Gautama was afforded unusual reverence by his followers.

More interesting for our present study, however, are references to Buddha's prescience of his approaching death. At Vesālī he told Ānanda that he would see the place no more:

'Now the Lord, having dressed betimes, took his bowl in his robe and entered Vesālī for alms; and when he had passed through Vesālī and had eaten his meal and was

[1] The others are, the Maha-Sudassana, a discourse which Buddha delivered on his death-bed, and the Jana-Vasabha, the story told by Buddha of the visit of Bimbisara to this world after death.

returning from the quest of alms, he gazed upon Vesālī with a leonine[1] look and addressed S. Ānando saying:

"Ānando, this will be the last time that the Tathāgato will look upon Vesālī." '

(Dīgha. II. 122.)

On the following day, when he was alone, Māra the Evil One came to Buddha and urged him to enter Nirvāna:

'Now not long after S. Ānando had gone, Māra the Evil One approached the Lord and standing beside him addressed him thus:

' "O Master, let the Lord now pass into Nirvāna,[2] let the Auspicious one pass into Nirvāna: now O Master, is the time for the Lord to pass thereto"; and moreover this word was spoken by the Lord: "O Evil One, I shall not pass into Nirvāna till my monks and nuns, my laymen and laywomen become wise and trained disciples, apt and learned, reciters of the Doctrine, walking in the Doctrine and the precepts, walking consistently, living out the precepts: until they have grasped the teaching for themselves, and shall announce and proclaim it, publish, establish and reveal, explain in detail and interpret, so that when a different system shall arise they may thoroughly refute it by the Doctrine and proclaim the "Doctrine with its miracles...." " And now, Master, is the Lord's religion spiritually strong, thriving, widespread, popular, ubiquitous—in a word, made thoroughly public among men. O master, let the Lord now pass into Nirvāna, let the Auspicious One pass into Nirvāna, now, O Master, is the time for the Lord to pass thereto."

[1] Pāli: 'elephant-look'; explained by Rhys-Davids as meaning that he turned with his whole body.
[2] 'parinibbatu', lit: 'become extinct'.

'When he had thus spoken, the Lord said unto Māra the Evil One: "O Evil One, be content; the Tathāgato's passage into Nirvāna will not be long: at the end of three months from now will the Tathāgato pass thereinto."

'Then the Lord, at the Capala shrine, mindful and conscious, laid down his term of life. And when his term of life was laid down by the Lord, there was a great earthquake, terrific and appalling, and the thunder[1] burst.

'When the Lord saw the event, he uttered upon that occasion the following Enunciation:

> "His principle of being, great and small,
> His term of life, the Sage laid down;
> Steadfast, with inward joy he broke,
> Like coat of mail, his own life-principle."'
>
> (Dīg. Nik. II. 104-107.)

When Ānanda returns he asks Buddha about the cause of the earthquake and the thunder, and is told that there are eight causes of earthquakes: in addition to the 'natural' cause, there are seven 'supernatural'. Among the latter are the conception, birth, and enlightenment of the Buddha, his turning of the wheel of the Doctrine, his shaking off his sum of life, and his attaining Nirvāna without any reminder.[2]

Buddha then tells him of Māra's visit and rebukes him severely for his failure earlier to ask Buddha to prolong his life for a cycle:

'If Ānanda, you had asked the Tathāgato, he might

[1] Lit: 'the divine drums'.
[2] It will be observed that this refers to a stage preliminary to the Buddha's entry into Nirvāna, and not to his physical death, which is to come three months later. But the decision to enter Nirvāna, the same passage makes clear, is final and irrevocable and physical death is merely a corollary of this decision.

have refused twice, but he would have assented the third time. Therefore, Ānanda, this was herein a fault of yours, this was an offence.'[1]

The events which led up to the physical death of Buddha and his full entry into Nirvāna are well known. At Pâvâ, near Kusinārā, Buddha ate a meal with Cunda, the smith, and after the meal was seized with sharp pain and vomiting. He set out, however, for Kusinārā with Ānanda, but had to rest by a tree on the way. He asked Ānanda to fetch some water, and Ānanda found that what was normally a muddy undrinkable stream had miraculously become pure and clean, and he took some water to the Buddha. (Dīgha II. 128-129.) It was at this time that there occurred the incident of the Transfiguration, already referred to. They went on, and reached Kusinārā, where Buddha was again forced to lie down. Though it was out of season,

'At that time the twin sal-trees were all one mass of blossom with untimely blooms', (Dīg Nik. II. 137-138),

and the flowers fell and covered his body, while divine mandârava flowers and sandalwood powder fell from the sky and divine music and singing sounded through the air in his honour. Buddha sent away Upavāna the Elder, who was standing before him fanning him, saying that so many gods were assembled to see him that there was no room for twelve leagues around and they were complaining that the monk obstructed their view. After some discussion with his followers, he gave them his last charge:

'Now then, monks, I address you; subject to decay are compound things: strive with earnestness.'
(Dīgha. II. 156.)

[1] Dīgha. II, 107-118.

Then he passed through the four stages of trance and attained Nirvāna, and—

'When the Lord entered into Nirvāna a great earthquake, terrific and tremendous, accompanied his entry into Nirvāna, and the drums of the angels rolled.'
(Dīg. II. 156.)

It is said that at this moment Brahmin Sahampati uttered the following lines:

> 'All beings in the universe
> Shall lay aside their compound state.
> Even so a Teacher such as he,
> The man unrivalled in the world,
> Tathāgata with the powers endowed,
> The Enlightened, has Nirvāna reached.'
> (Dīg. II. 157.)

Attempts the next day to carry Buddha's body south to cremate it are said to have been frustrated by the inability of the bearers to lift the body, and Anuruddha explained that the gods intended that it should go to the North. Immediately the whole town was covered with mandârava flowers which fell from the sky. At first the funeral pyre could not be ignited, and Anuruddha explained that the gods willed that the cremation should be delayed until the arrival of Kassapa the Great: when he did arrive, with his company of five hundred, and had done reverence to the pyre, it caught fire of itself. It burned without leaving behind any of the skin, flesh, sinews, or fluid of the joints, or any ash or soot. Streams of water came from the sky and extinguished it, and it was sprinkled also with scented water. (Dīg. II. 160 ff.) What is probably a later addition to the Sutta provides two lists of relics of the Buddha, which we are told were each enclosed in a stupa or shrine and venerated. Various attempts have been made to find the relics of the Buddha, and with doubtful success. What is of immediate interest however, is to note that by a very early date, probably before the time of the celebrated Buddhist king Asoka (c. 272-235 B.C.), there is evidence of a cult of the relics of the Buddha, and it may very well have developed soon after the Buddha's death.[1] The canon indeed suggests that this was in accordance with Buddha's express wish, for he is said to have charged Ānanda to treat his remains as they treat the remains of a king of kings.[2]

[1] Kathāvatthu XVII, 1, and see Thomas pp. 158-164, Keith, *Buddhist Philosophy*, p. 133, Oxf. 1923.
[2] Dīgha, II. 142.

SIX

HIS SUPERNATURAL CHARACTER

That Buddha was early regarded by his followers as being of a supernatural character and that they therefore reverenced him, is apparent both from passages in the canonical literature and from the early and later attitude of the Buddhists towards him. Some examples of the former may be given first. Thus a passage in the Anguttara Nikāya ascribes supernatural character to Buddha and puts the claim into the mouth of the Buddha himself:

'Once the Lord entered upon the main road between High-town and White-town. Now Dono the Brahmin entered it likewise. And he saw the wheels on the Lord's feet, with their thousand spokes, their tires and naves, and all their parts complete. Having seen them, he thought to himself: Wonderful and marvellous indeed! These cannot be the feet of a human being ... Upon seeing the hero (lit. the elephant) with his faculties at peace, he approached the Lord and said:

' "Are you not an angel?"
' "No Brahmin, I am not an angel."
' "Are you not a celestial genius?"
' "No Brahmin, I am not."
' "Are you not a goblin?"
' "No Brahmin, I am not a goblin."
' "*Are you not a man?*"
' "*No Brahmin: I am not a man.*"
' "If you are none of these, what are you then?"
' "Brahmin, those depravities (āsavas) wherefrom as an angel I should consider myself undelivered, are

for me renounced, uprooted, dug out, annihilated, unable to rise again in the future. And those depravities wherefrom as a genie, goblin or a man I should consider myself undelivered, are likewise renounced and uprooted. Monks (possibly a slip for O Brahmin), even as a blue lotus, a water-rose or a white lotus is born in the water, grows up in the water, and stands lifted above it by the water undefiled, even so, Brahmin, am I born in the world, grown up in the world and I abide, over-coming the world, by the world undefiled. *O Brahmin, you must call me a Buddha.*" '[1]

The simile of the lotus flower is found again in the Samyutta Nikāya:

'Monks, even as a blue lotus, a water-rose or a white lotus is born in the water, grows up in the water, and stands lifted above it, by the water undefiled: even so, monks, does the Tathāgato grow up in the world, and abide in the mastery of the world, by the world undefiled.'[2]

Evidently this attempt at setting the Buddha 'beyond the world' (lokuttaro) led to a sort of Buddhist Docetic controversy not altogether dissimilar from that recorded in the early centuries of the history of the Christian Church, for traces of it are to be found in a passage from the Kathāvatthu of the Abhidhamma:

'(You say) it ought not to be said that the Lord Buddha stood in the world of men?'

'Yes.'

'Are there not the Buddha's alms-rounds, the relic-

---

[1] Angutt. Nik. IV, 36: cf. II, 38, where a similar claim is made.
[2] Samy. Nik. XXII, 94.

shrines, the parks, lodges, villages, towns and cities, the kingdoms and countries?'

'Yes.'

'Well, then, if there be the Buddha's alms-rounds, relic-shrines, parks, etc., therefore assuredly it ought to be said that the Lord Buddha stood in the world of men. (Yet you still say) it ought not to be said that the Lord Buddha stood in the world of men?'

'Yes.'

'But was not the Lord born at Lumbinī and enlightened at the root of the Bo-tree? Was not the wheel of the Religion set rolling by the Lord at Benares; did he not lay down his term of life at the Capala shrine, and pass into Nirvāna at Kusinārā?'

'Yes.'

'Well then, it assuredly follows that the Lord stood in the world of men. (You still say) it ought not to be said that the Lord stood in the world of men?'

'Yes.'

'But was it not said by the Lord: "Monks, I once was staying at High-town, in Pleasant Grove, at the foot of the great sal-tree?" And again, "Once I was staying at Uruvelā, at the Goatherds Banyan tree, soon after my enlightenment", and again "I once was staying at Rājagaha, in the Bambu Grove, the Squirrels' feeding-ground"; and again, "Once I was staying, O monks, at Sāvatthī in the Victor's Grove, the cloister-garden of the Feeder-of-the-Poor"; and again, "Once I was staying at Vesālī, at Pagoda Hall in the Great Forest"? Is not all this Scripture (Suttanto)?'

'Yes.'

'Therefore indeed the Lord stood in the world of men (You now admit then that) the Lord Buddha stood in the world of men?'

'Yes.'

'Well then, if this be so, it must assuredly be said by us that the Lord Buddha stood in the world of men.'[1]

The Buddha is also said to have 'spiritual powers' over the angel-world:

'When a Tathāgato arises in the world, an Arahat, a Buddha supreme, endowed with wisdom in conduct, auspicious, knowing the universe, a matchless charioteer of men who are tamed, a Master of angels and mortals, a blessed Buddha; he preaches his religion: to wit, Personality (Sakkayo), the origin of personality, the cessation thereof, and the path that unto that cessation goes. And, monks, those angels of long life, self-radiant happy beings, abiding in the lofty mansions long, when they hear the preaching of the Tathāgato's religion, are everywhere seized with fear, astonishment and trembling, saying: "Impermanent are we, alas! O friend, 'tis said; and we thought we were permanent; unstable, and we deemed we were stable; non-eternal, who thought ourselves eternal. 'Tis said, O friend, that we are impermanent, unstable, hedged about with personality!"

'Such, O monks, is the spiritual power of the Tathāgato over the angel-world; such his great authority and mystic might.'[2]

Of even more precise significance are some of the titles of Buddha used in the canonical writings. Thus the

[1] XVIII. 1.
[2] Angutt. Nik. IV. 33.

Niddesa of the Khuddaka Nikāya discusses the meaning of the word 'deva'(god), and divides gods into three classes:

(1) gods by convention, i.e. kings, princes, and queens, 'deva' being a regular form of royal address.
(2) gods by birth, i.e. gods in the ordinary sense, from the four great kings up to the Brahma-gods and beyond.
(3) gods of purity, i.e. the disciples who are arahats and pacceka-buddhas.

The Lord himself, i.e. Buddha, is the god, the super-god (atideva), the god beyond the gods, (devātideva), over the conventional gods, over the gods by birth and the gods of purity.[1]

This last passage raises the question as to the precise nature of Buddha's divinity, and on this the opinion of scholars seems to vary. Thus Keith seems to believe that the Buddha either himself claimed or else allowed his followers to attribute to him, the kind of divinity which was at that time also being developed in connection with the great Indian gods, Çiva and Viṣnu. It is worth quoting Keith's conclusion at some length:

'It was the age of the growth of the great gods, Çiva and Visnu in their various forms, and the Buddha's success was due to the fact that he either had claims to divinity, or his followers attributed it to him and won general acceptance for the view. It is conceivable that divinity was thrust upon him against his will, but every ground of probability supports the plain evidence of the texts that he himself had claims which necessarily conferred upon him a place as high as the rank of the greatest of gods. The Buddha treats Brahmā, regarded as the highest of the gods, and all the hosts of heaven, with a cool super-

[1] See Thomas, *The Life of Buddha*, p. 214.

ciliousness which is explicable more easily on the ground of his conscious divinity than as an outcome of a rationalism, which certainly his disciples did not understand.'[1]

Thomas is rather more precise in his interpretation of Buddha's divinity. He says:

'It is thus possible to say that Buddha is called a god, but only in the sense in which the term god is defined by Buddhists. Every arahat has qualities that place him above the gods of current polytheism. But neither Buddha nor the arahat has become a god in the sense of the originator of the universe or its ultimate reality. Such a conception never appears, for the polytheistic standpoint remains in the doctrine that there have been many Buddhas, and in the view that all arahats are "gods", and even this classification of gods, which arose from the necessity of explaining the term "devātideva" never appears in the suttas.'[2]

While it now seems to be thus generally accepted that the earliest authoritative Buddhist scriptures portray the Buddha as divine,[3] it is equally clear that the same scriptures also portray him simply as a human teacher. A good example of what some of the early Buddhists thought about Buddha is found in the Dīgha Nikāya. Sonadanda declares that he is going to visit Buddha for the good report that he has heard of him. After describing the ascetic Gotama as well born on both sides for seven generations back, he says:

[1] *Buddhist Philosophy*, p. 29: Oxf., 1923.
[2] Op. cit., p. 214. He is referring, in the last sentence, to the passage quoted above from the Niddesa.
[3] Cf. Pratt, *Pilgrimage of Buddm.*, p. 6, N. York. 1928.
Cave: *Christianity and Some Living Religions of the East*, pp. 91-92: Lond. 1929.
James: *Comparative Religion*, p. 194: Lond. 1938.
Saunders, *The Gospel for Asia*, pp. 56-58: Lond. 1928.

'The ascetic Gotama has abandoned a great family circle. He has abandoned great wealth of gold (stored) both below and above ground. Even while a boy, a black-haired lad in the prime of youth, in the first stage of life he has gone forth from a house to a houseless life. While his unwilling mother and father wept with tear-stained faces he cut off his hair and beard, and donning yellow robes has gone forth from a house to a houseless life. He is beautiful, fair, attractive, with lovely complexion like Brahmā, in colour and presence not inferior to look upon. He is virtuous, of noble virtue, of good virtue, endowed with good virtue; of beautiful voice and speech, endowed with urbane will, clear and distinct for expounding the meaning. He is the teacher of the teachers of many, without lust, passion or fickleness. He teaches the brahmin race the doctrine of action and sets forth righteousness. He has gone forth from a high family, from an unbroken kshatriya family, from a family, rich, of great wealth, of great possessions. Men cross kingdoms and countries to come and ask him questions. Many thousands of divinities have taken refuge with him. This good report has gone abroad about him: "He is the Lord, the arahat, the fully enlightened, endowed with knowledge and conduct, who has well gone (sugata), the knower of the world, the supreme charioteer of men to be tamed, teacher of gods and men, the Buddha, the Lord." He is endowed with the thirty-two marks of a Great Man, offering welcome, friendly, polite, not frowning, speaking plainly and willingly. He is respected, honoured, revered and esteemed by the four assemblies. Many gods and men are devoted to him. In whatever village or town he enters non-human beings do not hurt him.'[1]

In this passage there is little to suggest that Buddha is

[1] Digha, I, 115-116.

divine, though there is obviously a tendency to attribute to him that perfection of wisdom and general character which may very well have been a contributory factor in the attribution to him of more than mere humanity. It is not, therefore, without some reason that an earlier generation of scholars tried to argue that the earliest view of Buddha held by his followers was that the Master was a great Teacher, but not more; and that the earliest conception of his message was an atheistic, semi-religious rationalism, which revolted against the severe monism of the Hindu Upanishads to assert that man and his moral life are the great realities. Oldenberg and Prof. and Mrs. Rhys Davids were the great exponents of this view. Thus Oldenberg declared, 'In his religion, the person of the Buddha has no place'.[1] Mrs. Rhys Davids has said: 'For me, the original teaching buried in what we have for less than two centuries called "Buddhism" was the work, the word, presence and life, of the North Indian "laird" known as Go'tāmā, son of Suddho'dānā and of Māyā. For me, during that life and for many years after it, "buddha" meant just no more than it does in the Upanishads, the spiritually wake or wise man. To all he was just the sāmānā Gotama.'[2] A similar attitude is reflected in a more recent essay by Professor Junjirō Takakusu, of Tokyo University, in which it is said: 'The Buddha was, after all, a man, but a man with perfect enlightenment. As a man he taught men to become like himself. Though people are apt to regard him as a superman, he did not regard himself as such. He was simply a perfected man. The Buddha did not deny

---

[1] *Buddha*, 4th Ed., p. 372.
[2] *What was the original Gospel in Buddhism?*, pp. 102-103: Lond. 1938. Cf. her comment in *Buddhism*, an earlier work: 'Surely a notable milestone in the history of human ideas that a man reckoned by thousands as the Light, not of Asia only but of the World, and the saviour from sin and misery, should call this little formula his Norm or Gospel.' p. 89: Lond., n.d.

the existence of gods (Devas), but he considered them only as the higher grade of living beings, also to be taught by him.'[1]

Professor Keith, however, as has already been noted above, has well disposed of this argument—at any rate so far as it is an attempt to use the evidence of the canonical writings. Probably we shall never know what Buddha thought about himself, but it is abundantly clear that the canonical writings reflect the view that Buddha was divine. Thomas may be right in saying that 'The earliest conception of the nature of Buddha that we find is that he was a human being', and that 'He comes to have superhuman attributes ascribed to him.' The important point is that, as Keith has said:

'The Vibhajyavādins[2] were plainly prepared to rationalize as far as practicable; as opposed to other Schools they minimize the supernatural element in Buddhism, and the salient fact is that even in the records of these would-be rationalists we find abundant proof that the orthodox and prevalent view of the Buddha made him far removed from ordinary humanity.'[3] 'The Pāli Canon contains no hint that even the greatest of Buddhist rationalists questioned the supernatural character of the Buddha.'[4] If therefore we are to base our conclusion firmly upon the canonical writings of Buddhism, there can be no possible doubt about the fact that divinity was attributed to the Buddha by Buddhists from the earliest period of which we have reasonable evidence.

[1] 'Buddhism as a Philosophy of "Thusness" '; Essay in *Philosophy East and West*, p. 85, ed. C. A. Moore, Princeton University Press, 1944; a volume of papers read at the East-West Philosophers' Conference held at the University of Hawaii during the summer of 1939.
[2] Traditionally said to have been declared 'orthodox' at a Council held in Asoka's reign: this School has been associated with the texts of the Pāli Canon which have come down to us.
[3] *Buddhist Philosophy*, p. 26.
[4] *Buddhist Philosophy*, pp. 28-29.

As has been pointed out by several writers, the acceptance of this fact makes it all the easier to understand how the later form of Buddhism—the Mahāyāna—which has taken such firm root in the Orient, could have developed its particular forms of Buddhology. The notion of the divinely worshipped Buddha-Saviour of the Mahāyāna is in fact the outcome of a further stage in the development of the divinity of Buddha which is already apparent in the early forms of the Hīnayāna. This development we must now notice in a little more detail.

SEVEN

BUDDHOLOGY OF THE MAHĀYĀNA

For a full account of the origins and development of the Mahāyāna or 'Great Vehicle', (sometimes known as Buddhism of the Northern School, in contradistinction to Hīnayāna, with which we have so far been concerned), reference must be made to some of the many authoritative works on the subject. Here it is sufficient to say that the Mahāyāna movement represented an attempt to relate the historic Buddha (Sākyamuni) to eternal Truth and Reality as a whole; it became effective in the first century A.D.; it rested largely on elements present in primitive Buddhism, while at the same time developed under strong influences from other aspects of Indian religion and philosophy. It took root in China, Korea and Japan and has found practical expression in a number of religious sects which still exercise a profound influence in those countries; indeed Arthur Lloyd's well-known book on Japanese Buddhism was called *The Creed of Half Japan*.[1]

The fundamental view which the Mahāyāna Schools and sects share about the nature of the Buddha is that, though the historical Buddha did indeed appear in the flesh, yet it is far more important to regard that historical manifestation as but one aspect—perhaps even the least important—of the essential Buddha-nature, which ultimately is to be conceived as the Absolute. The true nature of the Buddha is to be thought of as three-fold:

1. Nirmanakaya (Nirmana, transformation; kaya, body). As the human Sākyamuni who walked the

[1] London, 1911.

earth and preached to his fellows and passed away at eighty years of age.
2. Sambhogakaya (Sambho, enjoyment; bhoga, to partake; kaya, body). As the Buddha ideal who enjoyed a refulgent body and preached to the Bodhisattvas.[1]
3. Dharmakaya (Dharma, law, substance; kaya, body). As the highest being, comprising all others, the essence of knowledge and compassion, the Absolute.[2]

This doctrine of the three bodies of the Buddha (Trīkaya) in fact has its roots in the Hīnayāna. We find already in the Hīnayāna the conception of the distinction between the mere physical body of the Buddha which passes away, and the body of the law, which is the doctrine taught by him, to be realised by each man for himself. Later we find the idea that the material body of the Buddha is his body, while the law is his soul.[3] The law, however, which is the true nature of Buddha, is his insight or his enlightenment. Buddha himself suggests that at his death the law should take his place[4]; to know the law and all its implications is to know the Buddha. This identification of Buddha with his infinite knowledge paved the way for his identification with ultimate Truth and Reality as a whole: absolute knowledge cannot be other than Absolute Reality; hence the Buddha nature cannot fall short of the inclusive and ultimate Reality.

[1] Bodhisattva is the Mahāyāna equivalent of the Hīnayāna 'arahant', but whereas the arahant is one who has attained Nirvāna, the Bodhisattva has voluntarily laid aside his right to enter Nirvāna in order to work for the salvation of others.
[2] These are Mrs. Suzuki's definitions in her *Mahāyāna Buddhism*, pp. 40-41, Lond. 1938. Keith calls them respectively 'Magic Body', 'Body of Bliss' and 'Body of the Law'; See *Buddhist Philosophy*, pp. 267-272.
[3] Dīgha Nik. III. 84.
[4] Dīgha II. 124-126.

This final identification the Mahāyāna does not hesitate to make.

The doctrine of the Trīkaya was, however, also adumbrated by certain 'docetic' tendencies in the Hīnayāna which we have already noticed.[1] The so-called Third Council held at Patna in 256 B.C. condemned the views of those who held that Sākyamuni had never actually lived in the world of men, but had lived in the Tusita heaven, and had appeared on earth only in phantom form.[2] Moreover, the Pāli canonical writings, as we have also noticed, make Buddha himself refer to his existences on earth as a Bodhisattva which preceded his final appearance and entry into Nirvāna. Obviously, therefore, even in the Hīnayāna, the historic manifestation of Buddha was regarded as but an aspect of a whole series of manifestations—a point of view which is at the very base of the whole Trīkaya belief.

One of the earliest names to be associated with the Mahāyāna is that of Asvaghosha, who probably lived in the first or second century A.D. To him is traditionally ascribed the celebrated work known as 'The Awakening of Faith', in which the Dharmakaya is thus described:

'The eternal, the blessed, the self-regulating, the pure, the tranquil, the immutable and the free. Suchness is called the Tathagata's Womb (tathagata-garbha) or the Dharmakaya. The activity of the Dharmakaya has two aspects, the first depending on the phenomena-particularising consciousness by means of which the activity is conceived by the minds of common people, Sravakas and Pratyekabuddhas.

'The second depends on the activity–consciousness (Karmavijnāna) by means of which the activity is

[1] Chapter 6.
[2] This was the doctrine held by the Vetulyakas; see Keith, pp. 209, 221.

conceived by the minds of Bodhisattvas while passing from their first aspiration stage (cittopada) up to the height of Bodhisattvahood. This is called the Body of Bliss (sambhogakaya)'¹

The underlying thought here is that the Dharmakaya is to be identified with the ultimate cosmic principle (Bhutatathata)² which manifests itself on two lower planes, to ordinary people on the one hand and to bodhisattvas on the other. Mrs. Suzuki says that the Dharmakaya, as generally understood in the Mahāyāna, also corresponds to the Godhead in Christianity. For if on the one hand it denotes as 'Suchness', the Impersonal Absolute, yet on the other, as 'Womb of the Tathāgata', it is to be conceived as true knowledge, and the source of every individual being, underlying all phenomena, endowed with Love, Compassion and Will, and therefore personal.³

This, then, is what the Buddha is really and in himself. But owing to the fact that among finite beings there are all degrees of enlightenment and ignorance, the Buddha not only *is*, but *appears*. The finite beings to whom he appears are divisible into two great classes, namely, Bodhisattvas and all those who stand below them in enlightenment, including common people, Sravakas and Pratyekabuddhas. To each of these two classes the one Buddha has his characteristic form of appearance as body. The form he takes before the eyes of the blessed Bodhisattvas is the Sambhogakaya, while to the eyes of those on the lower plane he is manifested as Nirmanakaya.

'The Awakening of Faith' says:

¹ Quoted Suzuki, op. cit., p. 48.
² The usual English rendering is 'Suchness', though Pratt, in his *Pilgrimage of Buddhism* prefers 'Thatness' as indicating more clearly the idea of actuality behind the work. Keith suggests 'Thusness'. It seems agreed that it is meant to denote the ultimate, indefinable, cosmic principle.
³ Op. cit., p. 52.

'The Nirmanakaya depends on the phenomena-particularising consciousness, by means of which the activity is conceived by the minds of common people, Sravakas and Pratyekabuddhas. This aspect (of the Dharmakaya) is called Nirmanakaya (the Body of Transformation).'[1]

Of the Sambhogakaya Mrs. Suzuki says:

'The Sambhogakaya is visible to the Bodhisattva. It is a symbol of transcendental perfection and personifies Wisdom. It is the Buddha ideal. . . . The Sambhogakaya is the eternal Buddha, and many Mahāyānists turn to him rather than to the historical Sākyamuni, who is his mouthpiece or shadow. They have been blamed for this, but they retort that they prefer the substance to the shadow, the reality to the image.'[2]

Mrs. Suzuki, herself a follower of the Mahāyāna, naturally tries to present it in the most attractive light, and argues that this seemingly complicated belief is in fact no more difficult to understand than the Christian conception of God. The Dharmakaya is the Godhead in the philosophical sense; the personal Sambhogakaya corresponds to the God of the Christian believer; while the Nirmanakaya is to the Buddhists as Christ is to Christians. Whether this be an accurate parallel or no, the important point for the moment is to note the extent to which the Mahāyāna exalts the eternal Buddha as an object of veneration and worship, relegating the human Sākyamuni to a subordinate place as a manifestation of Reality. The culmination of this development can be seen in the work known as 'The Lotus of the Good Law', a work generally assigned to the period c. A.D. 500 and especially revered by the Tendai and Nichiren sects of

[1] Suzuki, op. cit., 43.
[2] Op. cit., pp. 45-46.

Japan. In that work it is said that Sākyamuni reached enlightenment, not first in Gautama's life on earth, but long before:

'Inconceivable are the thousands of Kôtis of Kalpas which have elapsed since I reached the supreme state of Bodhi, and since I have not ceased to teach the Law.

'Believing that my body has entered complete Nirvāna, they render diverse homages to my relics, and not seeing me, they long to see me.

'I see the utter destruction of men, and yet I do not show them my own form. But if perchance they yearn to see me, I expound the Good Law to those beings who thirst for it.

'Just so, I, who am the father of the world, self-existent being, I, the leader and doctor of all creatures, when I see them disposed towards contradiction, I show them my Nirvāna, although I have not as yet entered therein.'[1]

The theme of the 'Lotus' is the eternal Buddha; the Buddha whom the followers of the Mahāyāna adore is not the Sākyamuni of Kapilavastu, but the eternal Buddha. Pratt says piquently; 'Paraphrasing the words of St. Paul they might well have said, "Yea, though we had known the Buddha in the flesh, now know we him no more." '[2]

[1] Quoted from Steinilber Oberlin: *Buddhist Sects of Japan*, pp. 273-274, Lond. G. Allen & Unwin, 1938.
[2] Op. cit., p. 262.

PART II
THE PROPHET

A.H. = Anno Hijrah
A.H. 1 = 622 A.D

EIGHT

THE SOURCES

The sources of information for the life of Muhammad and for Muslim belief about his person are the Qur'an and the Traditions (ḥadīth), and it is important to remember that the latter rank with the Qur'an as, so to speak, 'canonical' or authoritative.

Whether the Qur'an was written down in full during Muhammad's lifetime is a question which cannot be answered with complete certainty. It is generally believed that its first compilation was made a few years after his death from pieces of parchment and leather, tablets of stone and other materials on which the revealed messages had been recorded. It seems clear, however, that in addition to whatever written records existed, several of the Companions of the Prophet preserved by heart and handed on their versions of the sacred revelations. What we do know is that under Othman, the third Caliph, who ruled from A.D. 644 to 656, an authoritative text was prepared at Medina and copies of it sent to the most important cities of the then Islamic world. Certain refinements and improvements in the orthography of the manuscripts were necessary but by the end of the first century the Arabic text as we know it today had been agreed upon and established: it seems clear that in this process the original form and contents of Muhammad's message were carefully preserved.

While the Qur'an, however, contains a record of the Prophet's messages and affords occasional insights into his character, it has little to say on the subject of Muslim belief about his person and from a comparatively early period Muslims have turned to Tradition for fuller information about the Prophet himself. Tradition may be said to have taken its rise during the lifetime of the Prophet, or at any rate, from the time of his death. The powerful influence of his personality upon his followers made believers want to know what the Prophet had done and said in various circumstances, so that they might emulate his example, and the six books of Traditions which Islam has elevated to canonical rank constitute this authoritative record. Professor Guillaume says of them:

'The *raison d'être* of this vast literature is to provide an authoritative standard of belief and conduct based upon the word and deed of Muhammad which shall be binding upon the whole of the Muhammadan world.'[1]

One of the most famous of the compilers of the accepted books of Traditions was Al-Bukhārī (A.H. 194-256), whose 'Ṣaḥīḥ' is probably the most highly esteemed. The account of his sixteen years' labour spent in making the compilation suggests that the process underlying the development and fixing of an Islamic 'canon' may have followed lines similar in some respects to those which are typical of the formation of the Buddhist and Christian canons. By the time that Bukhārī set to work it is clear that many thousands of ḥadīth or Traditions were known in the various Muslim communities. He is said to have travelled to places as far away as Balk, Merv, Misapur, the principal towns of Mesopotamia, the Hedjaz, Egypt, and Syria, in order to question over a thousand shaikhs about the Traditions which had been handed down to them. He is reputed to have examined altogether no less than 600,000 ḥadīth, from which he ultimately selected and preserved between 7,000 and 8,000. This

[1] *The Traditions of Islam*, p. 9: Oxford 1924.

gigantic task he undertook from pious motives: it is said that he always performed ablutions and offered prayers before deciding whether a Tradition was genuine or not. While we need not accept the figures here given as necessarily accurate, it is at least plain that a large number of ḥadīth were rejected as apocryphal and that the Muslim canon was fixed only as a result of a most careful sifting process.

A younger contemporary of Bukhārī, Muslim (ob. A.H. 261), also produced a collection of ḥadīth which, though not so highly esteemed as that of Bukhārī, is greatly valued and these two 'Ṣaḥīḥ' are the most important of all the recognised books of Traditions. The others are:

The 'Sunan' of Abū Dāwūd (*ob.* A.H. 275).
The 'Jāmi' of Al-Tirmidhī (*ob.* 279).
The 'Sunan' of Ibn Mādjā (*ob.* 273).
The 'Sunan' of Al-Nasā'ī (*ob.* 303).

Opinions differ as to the dates at which these Traditions were first written down. Obviously for a 'terminus a quo' we may go back as far as the lifetime of the Prophet himself but there is in fact no evidence which proves conclusively that any of them belong in their written form to such an early date. Sir William Muir was ready to accept the view that they were collected about a hundred years after Muhammad's death[1] but Professor Guillaume does not agree and says that 'The bulk of this literature is demonstrably the work of the two hundred and fifty years after the Prophet's death'. It seems clear, however, that the six canonical books of the Traditions were complete by A.H. 303 at the latest.[2]

The principle upon which ḥadīth were sifted by the

[1] *Life of Mahomet*, 4th Ed., Edinburgh 1923; Introd. xxxiv.
[2] Guillaume, op. cit., pp. 15 and 22-35.

compilers of the canonical collections was that of attestation by witnesses or 'guarantors'. From the outset ḥadīth were arranged under the name of the Companion of the Prophet on whose authority they were supported, irrespective of their contents. Attention was focused upon the chain of guarantors (isnād) going back to a Companion. To be reliable the 'isnād' always had to be in direct speech, so that an immediate link was thought to have been made with an indisputable authority and this was regarded as the most reliable guarantee of the trustworthiness of the Tradition. It will be realised that there is in this principle of selection a feature not unlike that which appears in the principles underlying the growth and fixing of the New Testament canon: the association of the canonical writings of the New Testament with one or other of the Apostles was clearly an important factor in their gaining acceptance by the majority of the early Christian communities.

The six books of canonical ḥadīth have been accepted as authoritative by the orthodox or Sunni Muslims and, for something like the first three centuries of Islamic history were so accepted by the whole of the Muslim world. The history of the emergence of the great Shiʻa schism in Islam is complicated: it was originally much more political than theological in character. For details of it the reader may be referred to any of the reputable histories of the religion.[1] During the first and second centuries of the Faith, however, orthodoxy gradually emerged from the teaching of the doctors of Medina, not however, without being partially influenced by certain Hellenistic and possibly also Persian ideas which it had encountered as Islam had spread through the lands of the Middle East. Gradually, however, the original

[1] A useful summary may be found in Gibb's *Mohammedanism*, Chapter 7; Oxford 1949.

political separatist tendencies of the S͟hī'a sect took on also a theological form and certain groups tended to build up their own interpretations of the Qur'an. This movement led eventually to the rejection by certain of the S͟hī'īs of parts of the Sunni Traditions and in the early part of the 4th century the first written collection of ''Alid' or S͟hī'a Traditions was compiled: it is known as 'Al Kāfī' and was composed by Al-Kulīnī, who died A.H. 328.

It will be necessary to take note of the fact that some of the ideas about the person of the Prophet which will be mentioned in the pages that follow are especially associated with S͟hī'a beliefs. Most of the beliefs, however, which are singled out for consideration were in fact held in common by the whole of the Muslim world of the first three centuries. In this connection attention may be drawn to the fact that one of the few English translations of a group of ḥadīt͟h, namely the Mis͟hkātu'l-Maṣābīḥ, derives from a well-known book of Sunni Traditions, still much used by Sunni Muslims in India. It was originally compiled by Al-Bag͟hawī, the celebrated commentator, who died A.H. 510 or 516. He called it the 'Maṣābīḥu 'l-Sunnah' or 'Lamps of the Traditions'. It was revised by Walīyu-l-Dīn Abu 'Abd Allah (*fl.* 737) who added an extra chapter to each section and called it 'Mis͟hkātu'l-Maṣābīḥ' or 'The Niche for Lamps'. It was translated into English by Captain A. N. Matthews and published in 1809: the translator arranged it in such a way that the various Traditions could be easily found and it is of great value.[1] Other quotations from ḥadīt͟h are taken from a variety of works, details of which are given in the text.

---

[1] Guillaume says there is some uncertainty about the complete trustworthiness of the text he used. Op. cit., p. 98 (note).

NINE

THE PRE-EXISTENCE AND BIRTH OF THE PROPHET

Tradition records that Muhammad was born about the year A.D. 570. There are, however, traces in the Traditions of the early growth of a belief in the Prophet's pre-existence. This is reflected, for example in two passages from the Mishkātu:

'Ab'u: "The Companions said: 'O messenger of God, when were you confirmed a Prophet?' He said, 'When Adam was between soul and body.' "

' Ib'ad-bin-Sa'riah: "Verily I was written near God the last of the Prophets; and verily Adam was in his own clay." '[1]

There seems little doubt that such a belief was current among the Sunnis and the Shī'īs but it became particularly significant in Shī'a teaching.[2] Koelle quotes the following Tradition from the biography of the Prophet, 'Rawzat ul Ahbab':

'Absolutely the first creature is the Light of our Prophet.... It is recorded that Meiserer ul Fejr narrated as follows: "I asked His Excellency the Prophet, 'When didst thou become a Prophet?' and he replied to me thus,

'When God created the great Throne and expanded the heavens and the earth, and placed the great Throne

---

[1] Mishkātu'l-Masābīh, trans. Matthews, Vol. 2, Ch. II, Pt. II, p. 659.
[2] North says: 'The idea of the essential pre-existence of the Prophet is current also among the Sunnis but not in the clearly articulated form that it has assumed in the development of Shī'a doctrine.' *An Outline of Islam*, p. 94, London 1934.

upon the shoulders of the angels who are the bearers of the Throne, He, by means of the Pen, wrote on the foot of the Throne, "There is no God but Allāh: Mohammed is the Apostle of Allāh and the seal of the Prophets.' " [1]

This conception of 'The Light of Muhammad' (in Persian the 'nūr-i-Muhammadī' and in its Arabic form 'Haqīqatu 'l-Muhammadīyah') was elaborated in the teaching of the Imām Qastalānī, who declared that it was related by Jābīr ibn 'Abdi 'llāh al-Anṣārī that the Prophet said: 'The first thing created was the light of your Prophet, which was created from the light of God. This light of mine roamed about wherever God willed, and when the Almighty resolved to make the world, he divided this light of Muhammad into four portions; from the first He created the Pen (qalam); from the second the Tablet (lauḥ); from the third the highest heaven and the throne of God ('arsh); the fourth portion was divided into four sections....' (He then describes how were created the firmaments, earth, paradises and hells, the light of the eyes, of the mind, of the love of the Unity of God, and the remaining portion of creation).

The author of the Hayātu 'l-Qulūb, a Shī'a book of Traditions, says:

'The holy light of Muhammad dwelt under the empyrean seventy-three thousand years and then resided seventy-thousand years in Paradise. Afterwards it rested another period of seventy thousand years under the celestial tree called Sidratu 'l-Muntahā, and, emigrating from heaven to heaven, arrived at length in the lowest of these celestial mansions, where it remained until the Most High willed the creation of Adam.'[2]

Sweetman says that one of the extreme Shī'a sects, the

[1] *Mohammed and Mohammedanism*, pp. 248-9: London 1889.
[2] Both these passages are given in Hughes, *Dictionary of Islam;* Art. 'Haqīqatu 'l-Muhammadīyah'; London 1885.

Mutaawidites, who flourished during the second century after the Hijrah, are held to have believed that God first created Muhammad and then committed to him the rule of the world. It was Muhammad and not Allāh who brought the universe into existence. Another version of the doctrine gave additional support to the Shī'a claim that the Imāmate descended through 'Alī and his successors, by teaching that the Light proceeded through Adam by Muhammad to 'Alī. Kumait (*ob.* A.D. 743) is said to have proclaimed this doctrine.[1]

The Shī'īs desired, of course, that the Imāmate should be reserved for 'Alī and his descendents, in whom would thus be combined the political and religious leadership of Islam. Meeting, however, with increasing resistance in the political field, they devoted themselves much more to the religious field. Among the ideas which gradually came to the fore in their teaching was the belief that in the Prophet and succeeding, legitimate Imāms there was present a manifestation of the divine. They accepted the two cardinal Muslim beliefs that Allāh is One and that the Qur'an is uncreated from all eternity but added a third, namely that the Imām specially chosen by God as the bearer of a part of the Divine Being is the leader to salvation. Many Shī'īs have believed that the divine element in the Imām passes to the next Imām, after the manner of the doctrine of transmigration. Since this manifestation of the divine was set forth in the Prophet himself, the Shī'a doctrine of the Prophet's pre-existence would seem to have followed quite naturally.

This Shī'a doctrine of the pre-existence of Muhammad was further developed by the Sūfīs, the mystics of Islam. In the place of the orthodox teaching on inspiration, which was content to declare that Gabriel transmitted all knowledge to Muhammad, they taught that Allāh

[1] Sweetman: *Islam and Christian Theology.* Pt. I, Vol. 2, p. 112. Lond. 1947.

revealed special wisdom and knowledge of some of His truths to the hearts of His elect. To Muhammad, however, was given all wisdom and knowledge, long before the creation of this world; it became part of his being long before he was sent to men.[1]

The Sūfīs distinguished between three grades of faith: believing first, that Muhammad was a prophet among the prophets; second, that he united in himself all the characteristics of prophets and became the prophet to the prophets; finally, the highest grade of faith ('fides specialissima'), Muhammad, when he received the revelation from God, received a part of God's being, and things were made known to him which remained secrets to the angels and even to Gabriel, the faithful spirit.[2] In this way, a recent writer declares in commenting on this development, 'The strength of faith in Muhammad became the measuring rod for the strength of faith in God, because there is no other way to God except through his intercession. Then Muhammad became the intercessor, the mediator.'[3]

The question arises how far the Shī'a ideas of the epiphany and the intercession[4] of the Imām are the direct continuation of similar ideas which, according to Ibn Ishāk (*ob. c.* A.H. 150), certain singers of primitive Islam already associated with the person of Muhammad —i.e. were current in Islam before the year A.H.11. The difficulty here is that in the present state of our knowledge it is almost impossible to say with any certainty precisely what influences played a part in assisting the growth of these and other related ideas. It is recognised by most scholars that Gnostic, Neo-Platonic, Manichaean and

[1] Tor Andrae, *Di Person Muhammads*, p. 308; Stockholm 1918.
[2] Tor Andrae, op. cit., pp. 310-312.
[3] Mr. Eric W. Bethmann in *Bridge to Islam*, Chapter 3; London 1953. See also Sell, *The Faith of Islam*, pp. 77-79; Madras, 1880. And Arberry, *Sufism*, p. 100; London 1950.
[4] See below, p. 110 ff.

old Iranian ideas have certainly intermingled with the earlier Muslim ideas, and, as will be noted later, Christian influence almost certainly played a part too.[1]

Whatever its origins may have been, however, there is no doubt about the fact that the belief in the pre-existence of the Prophet has had a considerable and lasting influence upon popular Islam. On this point, a recent writer who has spent over twenty years in Muslim countries in the Middle East declares:

'The tremendous influence which the Sūfīs had upon the masses through the different dervish orders should never be underestimated.... No one who ever witnessed or participated in the "maulid al nabt" celebrations, the festivities on the prophet's birthday (12 Rabī' al Awwal of the Muhammadan year), and heard the hymns and eulogies lavished upon Muhammad, will ever deny that Muhammad has taken the same place in the hearts of the Muslims that Christ has in the hearts of the Christians. In these eulogies we read that he is the Light of all light; he is the loveliest of all men; like a rose in a garden, like a pearl in the shell; through him all blessings flow.'[2]

A number of Traditions declare that the appearance on earth of the Prophet was not allowed to occur without the evidence of supernatural portents. Koelle refers to a number of passages in which it is said that soothsayers, diviners and jins (spirits) all prophesied the appearance of Muhammad: 'The prophecies of the Soothsayers and Diviners concerning the coming of that prince are also so many that we only give one as a specimen: Nazr Ibn Babia, one of the kings of Yemen, who is said to have been the builder of Samarkand and Herat, had a dream

[1] On all this see Art. Shī'a' in the *Encyclopedia of Islam*, Vol. IV, p. 350 ff., and Tor Andrae, op. cit., p. 314.
[2] Bethmann, op. cit., p. 40.

which frightened him. He gathered his soothsayers and astrologers to tell him the dream, as a guarantee for the correctness of their interpretation. They confessed that they themselves were not able to do so, but recommended Satih and Sak to be sent for, which was accordingly done. Satih stated that Nazr had seen in a dream a black-burnt substance, proceeding out of darkness, or out of a black cloud, and falling upon the land of Yemen, burning up everything in it. When Nazr had declared that such had really been his dream, Satih interpreted it thus: "Sixty or seventy years after Nazr's death, the Abyssinians will conquer Yemen. Then Seif Ibn Yazan will rise up and retake it from them. Then a pure prophet who receives revelations from the Lord of both worlds, will conquer it from the Yazanites; and in the hands of his people Yemen will remain till the day of the resurrection."[1]

The spirits (jins) also gave many prophecies of that prince's appearance. Abu Amir narrates that he went to Syria to inquire of diviners about the future, and says in his account, 'One moonlight night I fell asleep on my camel, which then went astray; and on awaking I found myself in an unknown wilderness, so that I was in great fear. Seeing several fires before me, I went towards them, when I perceived people around them who did not the least resemble men. They were warming themselves, and talking with each other in a loud voice, so that the hairs of my body stood up, and the camel in which I rode, stopped and began to tremble . . . One of them asked me, "Whence art thou?" and I answered, "I am from Ghazan, and am going to Syria, there to inquire concerning the future of the Diviners, and my name is Abu Amir." Then they made a sign to one of their number, saying, "Now is the opportunity." I turned

[1] Koelle, op. cit., p. 432.

towards him, and laid my request before him, remembering that the Diviners receive their information from the spirits (jins). That spirit said to me, "I swear by the rain that pours down from the clouds, and by those who people the waterless deserts, that thin-bodied, quickly-marching camels shall be brought to one who is the best of heroes, of covenant-keepers, of exhorters and commanders, and to whom word also shall be brought down from heaven. Surely the time is near, that one shall be called and raised up who will be a subduer of Caesars and Chosroeses." Then he described the form and beauty of that Excellency, and the seal of his prophetship, adding,"He shall be unlettered, and whosoever follows him shall find happiness. O Abu Amir, these things I have heard from the good angels with my own ears." [1]

It is said that calamities at the Persian court were interpreted by Parsi soothsayers as signs of the coming conquests of the Prophet and his followers:

'Sheikh Zarandi says, in his Book of Signs, that in the night of Mohammed's birth the courts of Chosroes parted asunder, and remained so till now, i.e. till A.H. 746 (A.D. 1368). Their remaining so is one of the greatest facts; and the great and adorable God alone knows how long they will still be left.'

'It is reported that, in the night of the birth of that prince, the sea of Sawa overflowed the land; and that the Wadi of Samawa, whose water had been stopped for a thousand years, began to be flooded with the waters of a great river, and the courts of Chosroes became shaking and trembling, and their fourteen towers fell to the earth. Chosroes seeing this, lamented and feared exceedingly; for he knew that these occurrences portended a national calamity. But, assuming an air of fortitude and courage,

[1] Koelle, op. cit., p. 433.

he kept his distress and trouble of mind concealed, for a while, from his people; and then made up his mind not to hide these occurrences any longer from his ministers of state and intimate friends. So he put on his crown, sat upon his throne, called a council, and when the élite of the people and his friends were assembled, there arrived a letter from his Persian empire. In this letter it was stated that the fires of the fire-temples of Persia, which for a thousand years had not been extinguished, but were continually burning, had gone out in a certain night, namely, in that in which also the towers of Chosroes' palaces had fallen down. This circumstance, therefore, still further increased Chosroes' grief and sorrow. A wise philosopher, also, the chief Judge, called the chief Fire-priest, said, "O Shah, I also have seen in a dream, on that night, that swift and indomitable camels were drawing Arab horses from the Tigris and were spreading over town and country." On hearing this from his chief Fire-priest, Chosroes said to him, "O chief Fire-priest, what is the interpretation of this dream? and what is to happen in the world?" The chief Fire-priest answered, "A great event is to happen in the direction of Arabia." [1]

Koelle also quotes the following Tradition which speaks of the appearance of a celestial light and of the sound of a heavenly voice at the Prophet's birth:

'Amina's midwife is reported to have said: "I was Amina's midwife: in the night when labour-pains seized her and Muhammad Mustapha fell into my hands, at his birth a voice reached my ears from the unseen world, saying, 'Thy Lord show mercy unto thee', and the face of the earth became so illuminated, from the East to the West, that I could see some of the palaces of Damascus by that light. Soon after that, darkness, fear and tremb-

[1] Koelle: op. cit., p. 256.

ling came upon me and then there appeared a light on my right hand, and in that state I heard someone from the invisible world say, 'Whither dost thou take him?' Another answered, 'I have taken him Westward to all the blessed and holy places and I have presented him to Abraham the Friend of God, who pressed him to his bosom, purified and blessed him.' " [1]

It is also recorded that God sent down, the same night, a host of angels to guard Amina, and keep her from the eyes of demons.

[1] Koelle, op. cit., pp. 254-257.

TEN

THE CALL

The Qur'an regards the first of the revelations of Allāh to Muhammad as itself constituting the Prophet's call to his prophetic ministry, but the Traditions take us back to Muhammad's boyhood and tells how, by the 'opening of Muhammad's heart', Gabriel cleansed him and sealed him for the ministry which was to come.

'Anas said, Verily Gabriel came down to His Majesty when he was playing with boys and took hold of him and laid him upon the ground and split his heart and brought out a little bag of blood; and Gabriel said: "This is the devil's part of you". After that, he washed His Majesty's heart in a golden vessel of Zem Zem water, then sewed it up, and replaced it.'[1]

Sūrah XCIV seems to contain a reference to this purification:

> 'Have we not OPENED thine heart for thee?
> And taken off from thee thy burden,
> Which galled thy back?
> And have we not raised thy name for thee?'[2]

Sūrah XCVII speaks of the descent of the Qur'an to the lowest heaven, whence it was gradually revealed to the Prophet:

> 'Verily, we have caused it (the Qur'an) to descend on the night of POWER.
> And who shall teach thee what the night of power is?
> The night of power excelleth a thousand months:

[1] Mishkātu, Vol. 2, p. 684.
[2] vv. 1-4.

Therein descend the angels and the spirit by permission of their Lord for every matter;
And all is peace till the breaking of the morn.'

The 'night of power', the celebrated 'Lailatu 'l-Qadr', seems to have been a recurring point of the year when the divine decrees were promulgated.[1] But to Muhammad it was one special night, when he received his first revelation. Sūrah LIII opens with what seems a fuller account of this beginning of revelation:

'The Qur'an is no other than a revelation
revealed to him: (i.e. Muhammad)
One terrible in power taught it him,
Endued with wisdom. With even balance stood he
In the highest part of the horizon:
Then came he nearer and approached,
And was at the distance of two bows, or even closer,—
And he revealed to his servant what he revealed.'[2]

The 'One mighty in power' evidently refers to Gabriel, whose name means 'The Mighty One of God', and, as will be seen below, Tradition generally regards the Qur'anic revelation as having been communicated to the Prophet by Gabriel.

Some have also interpreted Sūrah LXXIV in the light of this first revelation:

'O thou, ENWRAPPED in thy mantle!
Arise and warn!'[3]

---

[1] Tradition asserts that the revelation given on the night of power occurred in the month of Ramaḍān, and popular belief holds that on this night human destiny is determined for the whole year.
The date of the 'Lailatu 'l-Qadr' is not precisely indicated; therefore the nights of the days of odd numbers, from the 21st. to the 27th. of Ramaḍān, and especially this last day, are honoured by invocations and Qur'anic recitations.
[2] vv. 4-10.
[3] vv. 1-2.

And again, Sūrah XCVI:

> 'Recite thou, in the name of thy Lord who created:—
> Created man from CLOTS OF BLOOD:—
> Recite thou! For thy Lord is the most Beneficent,
> Who hath taught the use of the pen:—
> Hath taught Man that which he knoweth not.'[1]

Tradition adds further details about the 'Call' of the Prophet. It tells of Muhammad's terror at the appearance of Gabriel; how he communicated his fears to his wife, and how afterwards, during a period of doubt and depression, he actually contemplated suicide. Allāh, however, comforted and strengthened him and thereafter revelations came to him frequently. Of the various Traditions which deal with this subject we may quote two given by Muir from Al-Wāk̤idī:

'The first beginnings of Mohammed's inspiration were "real visions". Every vision that he saw was clear as the morning dawn. These again provoked the love of solitude. He would repair to a cave on mount Hira, and there pass whole days and nights. Then, drawn by affection for K̲h̲adīja, he would return to his home. This went on till the truth burst upon him in the cave. It happened on this wise. Wandering in the hills around, an angel from the sky said to him: "O Mohammed, I am Gabriel!" He was terrified, for as often as he raised his head, there was the apparition of the angel. He hurried home to tell his wife. "Oh K̲h̲adīja," he said, "I have never abhorred anything as I do these idols and soothsayers; and now verily I fear lest I should become a soothsayer myself." "Never," replied his faithful wife; "the Lord will never suffer it thus to be,"—and she went on to speak of his many virtues, upon which she founded the assurance. Then she repaired to her cousin Waraka, and told him

[1] vv. 1-5.

all. "By the Lord," cried the aged man, "he speaketh truth. Doubtless it is the beginning of prophecy, and there shall come upon him the Great Namus, like as it came upon Moses. Wherefore charge him that he think not aught but hopeful thoughts within his breast. If he be raised up a prophet while I am yet alive, surely I will stand by him." '

'Now the first Sura revealed to Mohammed was the 96th, verses 1-5, "Recite thou in the name of the Lord" etc.; and that descended on him in the cave of Hira. After this he waited some time without seeing Gabriel. And he became greatly downcast, so that he went out now to one mountain, and then to another, seeking to cast himself headlong thence. While thus intent on self-destruction, he was suddenly arrested by a voice from heaven. He looked up, and behold it was Gabriel upon a throne between the heavens and the earth, who said: "O Mohammed! thou art the Prophet of the Lord, in truth, and I am Gabriel." Then Mohammed turned to go to his own house; and the Lord comforted him and strengthened his heart. And thereafter revelations began to follow one upon another with frequency.'[1]

Leaving aside then, the various differences of detail in these quotations from the Qur'an and Tradition, it is generally believed that the prophetic work of Muhammad began with his Call, which is said to have occurred on the 'night of power', when he was summoned by Gabriel to receive the first revelation. That revelation may have come in dreams or by direct communication from Gabriel which Muhammad believed that he

[1] Muir, op. cit., pp. 49-50. For other references to Traditions about the beginnings of Muhammad's revelations see that of Abu Kuraib, quoted in Buhkhsh, *Studies Indian and Islamic*, Lond. 1927, p. 11: Mishkātu Vol.2, pp. 678-679, of Āyishah. Others given in Muir are of Ibn Hishām and Al-Tabarī. Muir also quotes a Tradition from Ibn Sa'd which suggests that the Prophet received the revelations with manifestations of mental and physical stress: see op. cit. pp. 50-52.

actually heard. What is agreed upon by all the traditions and apparently supported by the words of Sūrah LXXIV is that Muhammad's reactions to the first revelation were characterised by great fear and intense doubt, and that his self-confidence was ultimately restored only by the encouragement which he received from his wife Khadījah.

It would seem justifiable to refer to this aspect of the Call of Muhammad as his 'temptation', if by that term is to be understood the period of perplexity and distress which accompanied the first clear manifestation of a 'call' to prophetic office and which preceded the actual assumption of the work of a Prophet.

In this connection it is interesting to notice that the Muslim Traditions make no attempt to employ the notion of demonic opposition in the story of Muhammad's Temptation—a fact which strikes the casual reader as strange when he remembers that Islam has its 'Satan' who is mentioned several times in the Qur'an either as the 'Hater' (Shaiṭān) or the 'Calumniator' (Iblīs). A closer investigation of the nature of the 'Satan' in Muslim thought, however, reveals the fact that he is of much less immediate consequence for the everyday life of man than either the 'Māra' of Buddhism or the Christian 'Satan'. Though he represents, like them, the principle of evil, unlike them he is never allowed to withstand, even temporarily, the authority and power of Allāh, which are unquestioned and supreme. Moreover, men are predestined to evil as well as to good, and the Qur'an asserts plainly that it is Allāh Himself who leads men to the one or the other.[1] Within this framework of belief therefore, there is no room for the same kind of embodi-

---

[1] Iblīs is mentioned chiefly in connection with the story in the Qur'an of his refusal to worship created man: in Sūrah XV. 42 Allāh says to him: 'Over none of my servants shalt thou have power, save those beguiled ones who shall follow thee.'

ment of moral evil as that which is found in Buddhism, and Christianity: no Tempter therefore, approaches the Prophet as Māra does the Buddha and Satan the Christ; instead, Tradition tells a simple story of the Prophet's doubts and fears when confronted with the demands of Allāh himself.

Of the strong belief in Islam about the divine inspiration of the Prophet there can be no possible doubt. That Muhammad himself accepted these revelations as messages from God, and himself as the supreme and final agent or instrument of revelation, is clear from the Qur'an. Indeed it underlies the whole of the teaching of the Qur'an, and the passages quoted above may be taken as typical in this respect. Perhaps the most dogmatic utterance on this subject is in Sūrah XXXIII:

'Muhammad is not the father of any man among you, but he is the Apostle of God, and the seal of the prophets. ... O Prophet! we have sent thee to be a witness, and a herald of glad tidings, and a warner;

'And one who, through his own permission summoneth to God, and a light-giving torch.'[1]

Thus Margoliouth says of Muhammad:

'It is certain that a fundamental dogma of this system was the personal one that he was God's Prophet; agreement on other points presently became useless, if that were not conceded. ... Belief therefore in himself was the dogma which he taught himself first, and afterwards taught others.'[2]

Tradition, as we have also seen, naturally accepted this belief and emphasised it: it will be shown below how

[1] vv. 40 and 44.
[2] *Mohammed and the Rise of Islam*, pp. 77 and 79; 3rd Ed., Lond. 1923.

it actually magnified the Prophet's position until he became, not merely the Seal of the Prophets, but also the Supernatural Intercessor and Saviour of mankind.

ELEVEN

THE MINISTRY

(a) *The 'Night-Journey' (Mi'rāj') of Muhammad*
Sūrah XVII opens with the following words:

'Glory be to Him who carried his servant by night from the sacred temple of Mecca to the temple that is more remote, whose precinct we have blessed, that we might shew him of our signs! for He is the Hearer, the Seer.'

This is the only reference in the Qur'an to the celebrated 'Mi'rāj' or 'Night-Ascent' of the Prophet of which Tradition makes so much. It is said that on this night the Prophet ascended into heaven to hold communion with all the previous prophets, and, leaving Jesus far below in the second heaven, himself mounted to the seventh, and ate and drank with God. Al-Wākidī says that this journey took place on the 17th of Rabbī'u 'l-Awwal, twelve months before the Hijrah.[1]

The following account is taken from the Mishkātu 'l-Maṣābīḥ:

'Whilst I was sleeping upon my side, he (Gabriel) came to me, and cut me open from my breast to below my navel, and took out my heart, and washed the cavity with Zem-zem water, and then filled my heart with Faith and Science. After this a white animal was brought for me to ride upon. Its size was between that of a mule and an ass, and it stretched as far as the eye could see.

[1] See footnotes in Rodwell's Koran p. 164. Presumably it is on the strength of this Tradition that Muir puts this 'dream' of the 'night ascent' in the year 621 A.H.; op. cit. p. 121.

The name of the animal was Buraq. Then I mounted the animal and ascended until we arrived at the lowest heaven, and Gabriel demanded that the door should be opened. And it was asked "Who is it?" and he said, "I am Gabriel." And they then said, "Who is with you?" and he answered, "It is Muhammad." They said, "Has Muhammad been called to the office of a prophet?" He said, "Yes." They said, "Welcome Muhammad; his coming is well." Then the door was opened; and when I arrived in the first heaven, behold, I saw Adam. And Gabriel said to me, "This is your Father Adam, salute him." Then I saluted Adam, and he answered it and said "You are welcome! O good son, and good Prophet!" After that Gabriel took me above, and we reached the second heaven; and he asked the door to be opened, and it was said, "Who is it?" He said, "I am Gabriel." It was said, "Who is with you?" He said, "Muhammad." It was said, "Was he called?" He said, "Yes." It was said, "Welcome Muhammad; his coming is well." Then the door was opened; and when I arrived in the second region, behold, I saw John and Jesus (sisters' sons). And Gabriel said, "This is John, and this is Jesus; salute both of them." Then I saluted them, and they returned it. After that they said, "Welcome, good brother and good Prophet".... Then I entered the seventh heaven, and behold, I saw Abraham. And Gabriel said, "This is Abraham, your father, salute him"; which I did and he returned it, and said, "Welcome, good son and Prophet." After that I was taken up to the tree called Sidratu' l-Muntaha'. And I saw four rivers there; two of them were hidden, and two manifest. I said to Gabriel, "What are these?" He said, "These two concealed rivers are in Paradise; and the two manifest are the Nile and the Euphrates." After that I was shown the Baitu'l-M'amur. After that, a vessel full of wine, another full of milk, and another of honey were brought to me, and I took the milk and drank it. And Gabriel said, "Milk is religion; you and your people will be of it." [1]

Koelle refers to other Traditions which deal with the same incident and says of them: 'The narrators wish us expressly to understand that what they communicate was derived from their prophet's own lips.' In one of them Muhammad is supposed to have said:

'There appeared a green carpet ... and I was set upon it, and moved on till I reached the foot of God's Throne of Glory, and then was moved forward still further to the place of "Honour".'

Another account states that God said to Muhammad a thousand times, 'Come nearer to me' and that each time that prince was raised higher, until he reached the place of 'Nearness', and then that of 'Intimacy' whence he entered the innermost sanctuary, at a distance of two bow ranges; and then approached still more closely. Some Traditions then speak of Muhammad's conversation with Allāh.[2]

Of the significance of these Traditions of the 'Night-Ascent' of the Prophet to the very presence of God, Zwemer has declared that 'The Transfiguration of Jesus Christ is surpassed by the story of Mohammed's ascent into heaven.'[3] Though the framework of the story is patently unlike that of either the Buddha's 'Transfiguration' or that of the Christ, there is little doubt that the motive is similar. Muhammad is singled out as the successor of both Jewish and Christian worthies and even of Christ himself. Moreover as one who during his life-

---
[1] Mishkātu, Ch. VII, Pt. I, pp. 691 ff.
[2] Koelle, op. cit., pp. 304-314.
[3] *The Moslem Christ*, p. 162. Lond. 1912.

time has been allowed to enter into the very presence of God and hold intimate communion with Him, he is given a position which in fact makes him superior in dignity and honour to all the prophets who have gone before. This, of course, is in keeping with the general teaching of the Qur'an. Its significance is obvious, however, for the general development of the traditional Muslim view of the person of the Prophet: it was yet another step in the general direction of an increasing reverence for the Prophet which was to culminate in the ascription to him of a supernatural character.

(b) *The Miracles of the Prophet*

There seems to be a certain amount of doubt as to whether Muhammad actually claims in the Qur'an the power to work miracles. Thus, in the early days of the preaching, in replying to a demand from the Meccans that he should perform a miracle, the Prophet implies that he is unable to do so:

'And they say, "By no means will we believe thee till thou cause a fountain to gush forth for us from the earth;

' "Or till thou have a garden of palm-trees and grapes, and thou cause forth-gushing rivers to gush forth in its midst;

' "Or thou make the heaven to fall on us, as thou hast given out, in pieces; or thou bring God and the angels to vouch for thee;

' "Or, thou have a house of gold, or thou mount up into Heaven; nor will we believe in thy mounting up, till thou send down to us a book which we may read." SAY: Praise be to my Lord! Am I more than a man, an apostle?"[1]

[a] Sūrah, XVII, 92-95; cf. XVII, 61, and XXIX, 49.

Nevertheless, it is clear that in fact even the Qur'an itself does suggest that Muhammad had the power to work miracles. The miracle 'par excellence' was the Qur'an itself.[1] the Prophet declares it to be a direct message, or series of messages, from Allāh. Muhammad is credited with the ability to foretell the defeat of the Persians by Heraclius, and the fulfilment of this prophecy is regarded by Muslims as clear evidence of the inspiration of the Prophet.[2] The plainest allusion, however, is to be found in Sūrah XLIV 1-2, which refers to the miracle of the 'Splitting of the Moon'.

> 'The hour hath approached and the MOON hath been cleft:
> But whenever they see a miracle they turn aside and say,
> This is well-devised magic.'

Tradition has supplied fuller details of this miracle. It is said that Abū Jahl and a Jew visited the Prophet and demanded a sign from him on pain of death. The Prophet made a sign with his little finger, and at once the moon separated into two parts: one of which remained in the sky, the other went off to a long distance. The Jew believed in Islam forthwith. Abū Jahl ascribed the affair to magic, but on making enquiry from various travellers, ascertained that they, on this very night, distinctly saw the moon in two parts.[3]

[1] In the Mishkātu, Abū Hurairah testifies that Muhammad declared: 'There is no Prophet but was given miracles, which when the sects saw they believed; ... and my miracle is the Koran, which was sent to me and will remain for ever.' Ch. II, Pt. I, p. 656.

[2] Sūrah, XXX. 2 f.

[3] This version is from a tradition quoted in Sell, *The Faith of Islam*, pp. 158-159. Reference is also made to it in a Tradition quoted in the Mishkātu, Ch. II, Pt. II, p. 684.

'Anas said: The people of Mecca asked His Majesty to show them miracles to prove the truth of the prophecy; and he showed them the moon split in two and the mountain of Hira between.' (p. 684). This version of it would seem to be a general contradiction of the contention of Sūrah XVII, quoted above.

Whatever uncertainty there may be, however, in the Qur'an as to the Prophet's miraculous powers is swept away in the Traditions, which credit him with a number of miracles of various kinds. Mention is there also made of other miracles ascribed to the direct intervention of Allāh in furtherance of the Prophet's witness. For convenience they may all be considered together under the following heads:

(1) Miracles of the Hijrah.
(2) Miracles of the Preaching.
(3) Miracles in Battle.

(1) *Miracles of the Hijrah.* The Prophet's flight from Mecca to Medina in A.D. 622 took place in the evening. With Abū Bakr he made his way south and, clambering up the rugged slopes of Mount Thaur, about one and a half hour's journey from the city, took refuge from search-parties in a cave near its summit.[1] Tradition meanwhile says that Subakreh's house was cursed by Muhammad, and fell to the ground, thus preventing Subakreh from capturing Muhammad as he fled.[2] Around the story of the Cave, however, there have grown up several stories of miraculous happenings to explain how Muhammad's life was there divinely preserved. A spider wove its web across the entrance. Branches sprouted, covering it on every side. Wild pigeons settled on the trees to divert attention. The following account from Muir gives the version of Al-Wākidī:

'Al-Wākidī says that after Mohammed and Abū Bekr entered, a spider came and wove her webs over the mouth of the cave. Koreish hotly searched after Mohammed in all directions, till they came up to the entrance. When they looked, they said: "Spiders' webs are over it

[1] Reference is made to this event in Sūrah IX. 40.
[2] Mishkātu, p. 697.

from the birth of Mohammed" ' and so they turned back. Again, 'God commanded a tree and a spider to cover the Prophet, and two wild pigeons to perch at the entrance of the cave. When a company of two men from each clan of the Koreish, armed with swords pursuing the Prophet, were now close to him, the foremost saw the pigeons, and returned to his companions, saying that he was sure from this that nobody was in the cave. The Prophet, hearing his words, blessed the pigeons, and made them sacred ever after in the Holy Territory, where it is sacrilege to harm them.'

A somewhat later Tradition tells how Abū Bakr put his hand into the crevices of the cave to remove the snakes that might be lurking there, and was unharmed by their venomous bites.[1]

When they eventually reached Medina safely, Muhammad was greeted by crowds of the inhabitants and received many offers of lodging. He avoided controversy and jealousy by deciding to stay wherever his camel stopped, and she finally entered a courtyard near to the house of Aby Eiyub. Tradition adds the following details, intended to invest the event with a supernatural air:

'Mohammed having left the halter quite loose, Al-Kaswa got up again and went a little way forward; perceiving her error, she returned straightway to the self-same spot, knelt down, and, placing her head and neck on the ground, refused to stir.'[2]

(2) *Miracles of the Preaching.* The following Traditions occur in the Mi<u>sh</u>kātu and all have reference to alleged miraculous events which in one way or another helped

[1] Muir, op. cit., 139-140.
[2] See Muir, op. cit., 170 note 2.

to confound unbelievers and to help forward the preaching of the Message of Islam.

(i) Al-Barā Ibn 'Azib is said to have recounted how one, Abdullah, in attacking an opponent, broke his leg, and then tells how Abdullah declared:

'Then I reached the Prophet and informed him of it and he said Stretch out your leg, which I did, when he passed his blessed hand over it and it was cured; you might say that I never had felt any pain in it.'[1]

(ii) Stony ground made sand. 'Jabir said, We were digging a trench ... and came to hard ground which it was not easy to dig ... and His Majesty took up an axe and struck the hard ground which became a heap of sand.'[2]

(iii) The Feeding of the Thousand. Jabir: 'O Messenger of God I have killed a kid and my wife made flour; come and the party with you.' And His Majesty said 'Do not take off your kettle, nor bake your flour till I come'. Then His Majesty came and my wife brought out to him the flour which she had and His Majesty spit into it and prayed for blessings on it and increase. After that he came to the kettle and spit into it and prayed for blessings on it and increase; and said to my wife, 'Call another woman to take along with you and take the meat out of the kettle with a spoon but do not take off the kettle'. Jabir says, 'The people of the trenches were one thousand and I swear by God they ate and went away having, and verily my kettle boiled as it was and my dough continued baking as at first.'[3]

(iv) Other 'Nature Miracles'. Jābir reports that Muhammad removed two trees 'like a camel led along with a rope in its nose' to give him shade.[4]

[1] pp. 700-701.   [2] p. 701.   [3] pp. 701-702.   [4] Mishpātu 703.

Muhammad curses the grave of an apostate and though buried several times the earth would not retain him.[1]

Abundant rain was produced by Muhammad's prayer at a time of drought.[2]

Jābir's father's creditors received in payment dates which had been miraculously increased from a few by Muhammad.

Butter, part of which Muhammad had eaten, increased continually.[3]

Seventy or Eighty people were fed on a few barley loaves and a little butter, after Muhammad had prayed for a blessing upon it.[4]

A tree moved from its place of its own accord and shaded Muhammad while he slept.[5]

A tree bore witness to Muhammad saying, 'It is as His Majesty said.'

A wolf spoke and converted a Jew.[6]

Muhammad discerned poison in some mutton, saying that the mutton had told him of a Jewess's plot to kill him.[7]

(v) *Other 'Healing Miracles'*. Muhammad healed a severe wound in the leg of Salmah by blowing upon it.[8]

A maniacal boy was cured by Muhammad rubbing his hand over the boy's breast and praying.[9]

(3) *Miracles in Battle*. Tradition describes how a number of miraculous happenings took place during some of the great battles of the early days of the sacred wars of the Prophet and his followers. Among them the celebrated Battle of Badr, which saw the defeat of the Meccan army, has understandably given rise to a considerable number.

The Qur'an itself alludes in several places to the

[1] Mishkātu 708.   [4] Mishkātu 712.   [7] Mishkātu 720-721.
[2] Mishkātu 709.   [5] Mishkātu 718.   [8] Mishkātu 704.
[3] Mishkātu 711.   [6] Mishkātu 719.   [9] Mishkātu 718.

strengthening of the Muslim army by a force of a thousand angels:

'When ye sought succour of your Lord, and he answered you, "I will verily aid you with a thousand angels, rank on rank."

'And God made this promise as pure good tidings, and to assure your hearts by it for succour cometh from God alone! Verily God is Mighty, Wise.'[1]

'Ye have already had a sign in the meeting of the two hosts. The one host fought in the cause of God, and the other was infidel. To their own eyesight, the infidels saw you twice as many as themselves: And God aided with his succour whom He would: And in this truly was a lesson for men endued with discernment.'[2]

Moreover, the help which Satan had intended for the Meccan army was frustrated by Allāh:

'When Satan prepared their works for them, and said, "No man shall conquer you this day; and verily I will be near to help you": But when the two armies came in sight, he turned on his heel and said, "Ay, I am clear of you: ay, I see what ye see not: ay, I fear God; for God is severe in punishing." '[3]

Tradition develops these notions still further and there are endless legends about this angelic intervention. The Devil is said to have appeared in the favourite form of Ibn Suraka and he is said to have been seen running from the field of battle, while in fact it was the Devil. It is said that one of the enemy suddenly perceived a tall white figure in the air, mounted on a piebald horse; it was an angel who had bound his comrade, and left him

---
[1] Sūrah VIII, 9-10. In Sūrah III, 120; the number of angels is given as 3,000.
[2] Sūrah III, 11.
[3] Sūrah VIII. 50.

on the spot a prisoner, and this was the cause of his conversion.¹

From the Mishkātu come stories of other miracles which occurred in the battles of the Faith:

'Jabir said On the day of the battle of Hadnibiah the men were thirsty and there was a leathern bottle near His Majesty, and he did Wadu from it. After that the men turned themselves to him and said We have no water to drink, or for Wadu; except that which is in your bottle. Then His Majesty put his hand into it and water spouted from between his fingers, like fountains. Jabir says Then we all drank and performed Wadu and I was asked How many of you were there? I said ... we were five hundred.'²

'Muhammad poured a pot of water into a well which was empty and prayed for abundance and left it for an hour. Then fourteen hundred men and their horses drank from it.'

Muhammad called for two water skins from a passing woman and watered forty of his men and yet the skins remained full as at first.³

Medina is said to have been guarded by angels during Muhammad's absence.⁴

Another account is given of how Muhammad supplied water from between his fingers.⁵

There was a miraculous increase of the water in a pot and a hundred thousand men were fed with a few frag-

---

[1] Muir, op. cit., pp. 235-236 note. The Mishkātu quotes Ibn Abbas as saying that Gabriel and the angels succoured the faithful at the Battle of Badr, p. 700. Of the significance of the Battle Margoliouth has said: 'No event in the history of Islam was of more importance than this battle ... Its value to Muhammad himself it is impossible to overrate; he possibly regarded it himself as a miracle and when he declared it one, most of his neighbours accepted the statement without hesitation.' (Op. cit., p. 269).

[2] Mishkātu, p. 702. [4] Mishkātu p. 709.
[3] Mishkātu p. 703. [5] Mishkātu pp. 712-713.

ments of food. Three hundred were fed from a single cake.¹

Professor Guillaume has devoted several pages of his book, *The Traditions of Islam*, to showing that the stories of the miracles of Muhammad were borrowed by 'a certain group of traditionists and theologians' from Christian sources. He suggests that their motive was to enable the Prophet of Islam to compete with the Christ:

'Not content with the picture of a courteous, kindly, and able man, famed as the possessor of all human virtues, the idol of his race, if he was to compete with the Messiah they must represent him as a worker of miracles.'

He refers to the testimony of a certain Al-Kindī, who lived in either the 9th or the 10th centuries A.D., and who was an early apologist for Christianity against Islam,² in support of this argument:

'It is interesting to notice that apparently the only miracles said to have been performed by Muhammad and known to al-Kindī are: the wolf and ox that spoke; the tree that moved towards the prophet—the shoulder of goat's flesh, poisoned by Zainab bint Ḥārith the Jewess, which called out that it was poisoned; and the miraculous production of water. Some, this writer says, the Aṣḥābu-l-Akhbār reject altogether, while others are from reporters branded 'ḍa'īf.' (i.e. as those who recount fables).

He suggests that there are four obvious types of borrowing of miracle-stories from Christian sources:

(1) The Feeding of the Thousand, from the Christian story of the Feeding of the Five Thousand.

(2) The story of the healing by the Prophet of

[1] Mishkātu, pp. 713-714.
[2] See Sweetman, *Islam and Christian Theology*, Vol. I, p. 66; Lond. 1945.

Salma's wounded leg, from the story of Christ's healing of the deaf mute (Mark vii. 33).

(3) The story of the healing of the woman's demoniac son, from the story of the man possessed of an unclean spirit.

(4) Certain stories in which the Companions of the Prophet benefit by miraculous happenings, as do the Apostles in the New Testament.[1]

It is interesting—and for the present argument important—to notice that at this comparatively early date in the history of Islam Al-Kindī, an avowed opponent of the Faith, provides clear evidence of the fact that the Prophet is generally credited by his followers with the possession of miraculous powers. Sweetman points out, moreover, that though Al-Kindī rejects the claim of Islam that its Prophet worked miracles, a 'counterblast' from the Muslim side was provided for in the work of Al-Ṭabarī, who asserts against Al-Kindī that miracles were performed by Muhammad:

'The Night Journey. Lahab was miraculously eaten by a lion, at the word of the Prophet. Walīd b. Mughīra met him and the Prophet made a sign to a wound he had in the sole of his foot and it broke out and killed him. Then Aswad b. 'Abd Yaghūth met him and the Prophet made a sign to his belly; and he became dropsical and died. A camel and a calf spoke to him and a wolf gave testimony of his prophethood. Trees walked at his command. He miraculously provided water.'[2]

There can therefore be no doubt at all that the miracle-stories in Muslim tradition, of which some account has been given in these pages, represented a very real and

---

[1] Guillaume, op. cit. pp. 132-138. See also the article ' Muhammad' in the *Encyclopedia of Islam*, Vol. III, p. 657.
[2] Sweetman, op. cit., Vol. I, p. 70.

important part of a widely accepted Muslim body of belief about the person of the Prophet at a comparatively early date in the history of Islam.

The evidence that is available seems to indicate, however, that Islam shared with Christianity a belief in the evidential value of miracles as part of the 'bona fides' of the true prophet, and did not simply import into its traditions certain of the miracle-stories of Christianity. This is not to suggest that the miracle-stories in the Traditions of Islam have not been influenced by those found in Christian sources; in view of the early and considerable influence upon Islam of both Christianity and Judaism, it would be remarkable if this had not been the case, and the parallels in many cases are too obvious to be explained satisfactorily in any other way. But Islam was, as Sweetman has made clear, a virile religion which had its own view of the significance of miracle from the earliest period. And though its miracle-stories may have developed in scope or even in number as a result of the influence of similar Christian stories, the essential belief in the miraculous powers of Muhammad was already in existence to make such development possible and also congruous with the general outlook of Islam.

TWELVE

THE DEATH OF THE PROPHET AND HIS HEAVENLY INTERCESSION

In the month of May in the year A.D. 632 (A.H. 11) Muhammad became ill with a violent headache and high fever. He was nursed by his favourite wife Āyishah but died in the early part of the following month. After the final rites had been performed, the Prophet was buried, in the presence of a vast concourse of the faithful, in a grave which had been dug in the house of Āyishah where he had died.

Tradition has embellished the story of the Prophet's last days with descriptions of marvellous events which are plainly intended to testify to the supernatural significance of his death.

Thus, a Tradition recorded in the Mishkātu tells how the Prophet foretold his death.

'Verily I am going before you and will bear witness of your obedience and accepting Islam.'[1]

It is said that when the 110th Sūrah was revealed Muhammad called Fāṭimah and said:

'My daughter! I have received intimation of my approaching end.' Fāṭimah burst into tears. 'Why weepest thou, my child?' continued the prophet; 'be comforted, for verily thou art the first of my people that shall rejoin me.' Whereupon Fāṭimah dried her tears and smiled pleasantly.[2]

Another Tradition tells how the Prophet is said to

[1] Mishkātu p. 732.   [2] Muir, p. 482, note 2.

have declared that he had deliberately chosen to meet his Lord.

'The choice hath verily been offered me of continuance in this life, with Paradise thereafter, or to meet my Lord at once; and I have chosen to meet my Lord.'[1]

A similar declaration by the Prophet is said to have been made also to the people assembled in the Mosque, and its significance to have been perceived only by Abū Bakr, who burst into tears:

'Verily, the Lord hath offered unto one of his servants the choice between this life and that which is nigh unto Himself; and the servant hath chosen that which is nigh unto his Lord.'[2]

Yet another Tradition referred to by Muir, tells how angels and angelic voices pronounced incantations over the dying Prophet and also lamented his approaching death:

'Three days before the death of Mohammed, Gabriel came down to visit him: "O Ahmed!" he said, "the Lord hath deputed me thus as an honour and peculiar favour unto thee, that He may inquire concerning that which indeed He knoweth better than thou thyself: He asketh, 'How thou findest thyself this day?' " "Gabriel!" replied the Prophet, "I find myself in sore trouble and agony." Next day, Gabriel again visited Mohammed and accosted him in the same words: Mohammed replied as before. On the third day Gabriel descended with the Angel of Death; and there also alighted with him another angel, Ismail, who inhabiteth the air, never ascending up to heaven, and never before having descended to the earth since its creation: he came now in command of 70,000 angels, each in command of 70,000 more. Gabriel, preceding these, addressed

[1] Muir, p. 483. [2] Muir, p. 485.

Mohammed in the same words as before, and received the same reply. Then said Gabriel: "This, O Mohammed! is the Angel of Death. He asketh permission of thee to enter. He hath asked permission of no man before, neither shall he ask it of any after thee." Mohammed gave permission so the Angel of Death entered the room, and stood before Mohammed, and said: "O Ahmed, Prophet of the Lord! Verily God hath sent me unto thee, and hath commanded me to obey thee in all that thou mayest direct. Bid me to take thy soul, and I will take it; bid me to leave it and I will do accordingly." To which Mohammed replied: "Wilt thou, indeed, do so, O Angel of Death!" The angel protested that his mission was even so, to do only that which Mohammed might command. On this Gabriel interposed and said: "Oh Ahmed! verily the Lord is desirous of thy company". "Proceed, then," said Mohammed, addressing the Angel of Death, "and do thy work, even as thou art commanded." Gabriel now bade adieu to Mohammed: "Peace be on thee," he said, "O Prophet of the Lord! This is the last time that I shall tread the earth; with this world I have now concern no longer." So the Prophet died; and there arose a wailing of celestial voices (the sound was audible, but no form was seen) saying: "Peace be on you, ye inhabitants of this house, and mercy from the Lord and his blessing! Every soul shall taste death." "[1] [2]

[1] Muir, pp. 494-495, note 4.
[2] Koelle reports other Traditions, one of which tells how Gabriel told Muhammad that the flames of hell had been extinguished; the spirits have dressed, and the black-eyed houris have adorned themselves, and the angels have formed lines to meet his spirit. No other prophets or their people will enter paradise till he and his people have entered. God has given him the pond of nectar, the lauded place, the intercession on the day of resurrection, and many of the people. Āyishah is reported to have said that when Muhammad died there was observed such a sweet fragrance as had never before been perceived by any of the Meccan travellers. 'Ali is reported to have said that he heard a voice from the corner of the house saying 'O Muhammad'. 'Ali told others of the house who heard the voice 'It is the voice of a messenger from the unseen world who has come to comfort us'. Koelle, op. cit., 367-368.

Thus it may be said that Tradition invests the death of Muhammad with more than natural and more than human significance: it is an event deliberately decided and not—as with ordinary mortals—unpredictable and uncontrollable. The Prophet's passing, moreover, is marked by heavenly visitations, which help to give to it a supernatural significance. Thus Margoliouth says that part of the purpose of these Traditions is 'to glorify the Prophet, and make his death, if not the result of choice, at least foreknown.'[1]

There are also a number of Traditions which purport to describe miraculous events connected with the tomb of the Prophet.

Thus, it is said that many of Muhammad's Companions chose to remain in Medina after his death, in order to comfort themselves by visiting his grave. 'When they had any difficulty they used to come and stand over against his sepulchre, and then were caused to hear an answer from that Excellency, solving their difficulties; to some of them it was given to hear it with the ears of their body; to others with the ears of the soul. That prince's sepulchre was exceedingly bright and extremely light and shining. Those who did not see His Excellency openly, but merely his illumined tomb, used to bear witness that he who lies in that tomb must be a prophet.'[2]

Another Tradition describes how a penitent Arab heard from the tomb a voice which proclaimed the pardon of his sins:

'It is recorded on the testimony of Ali that three days after his Excellency's funeral there came an Arab, who threw himself down upon the prince's grave, and took a handful of earth from it, casting it upon his own head, and then called out, "O Apostle of God, thou hast spoken

[1] Op. cit., p. 468.   [2] Koelle: op. cit., p. 372.

it, from thee we have heard it, thou hast received it from God, and we have received it from thee, and it is derived from those who came down to thee, that noble verse, 'And if they have darkened their souls, let them come unto thee!' I have brought darkness on my soul: but I am come to thee as a confounded, bewildered sinner, that thou mayest ask pardon for me of the Most High." Then there came forth a voice from that Excellency's tomb, saying three times, "Thou hast been pardoned, thou hast been pardoned." [1]

It will be noticed that this last Tradition introduces a new element—the suggestion that the Prophet can act as an intermediary between Allāh and the believer. In fact, Tradition has built up a belief in the power and efficacy of Muhammad's intercession at the Last Day which is evidently of considerable significance in popular Islam. It is doubtful whether such a belief can be found in the Qur'an. Sūrah XXXIX. 45 seems to make it clear that intercession is limited to God Himself:

'Say: Intercession is wholly with God: His the kingdom of the Heavens and of the Earth! To him shall ye be brought back hereafter!'[2]

Similarly Sūrah VI. 51 certainly seems to exclude any idea of intercession by the Prophet:

'And warn those who dread their being gathered to their Lord, that patron or intercessor they shall have none but Him, to the intent that they may fear Him!'[3]

However, another passage has been made the foundation of the development in Tradition of the belief that

[1] Koelle: op. cit., p. 373.
[2] It may be noticed, however, that Rodwell, in a footnote to this verse in his translation of the Qur'an, seems to suggest that it means that only those may intercede with Allāh whom He permits to do so: p. 258, note 3.
[3] Cf. also VI, 69, and XXXII, 3.

Muhammad has been appointed as an Intercessor for men:

'Thy Lord will raise thee (Muhammad) to a laudable station.'[1]

Sweetman quotes a Tradition in which the Prophet is reported as having declared:

'My intercession shall be on behalf of those of my community who have committed mortal sins.'[2]

Similarly other Traditions recorded by Abū Hurairah say:

'The Prophet said: "I will also put on a dress and will stand near the throne, where no one else will be allowed to stand and God will say: 'Ask and it shall be granted to thee; intercede, thy intercession shall be accepted.'"'[3]

Sell's summary of this aspect of the Traditions is worth quoting in full; he says:

'The orthodox belief is that Muhammad is now an Intercessor and will be so at the Last Day. The intercession then is of several kinds. There is the "great intercession" to which the words, "it may be that thy Lord will raise thee to a glorious station," (Sūrah XVII. 81) are supposed to refer. The Maqám-i-mahmúd (glorious station) is said to be the place of intercession in which all persons will praise the Prophet. The people will be in great fear. Muhammad will say, "O my people! I am appointed for intercession." Their fear will then pass away. The second intercession is made so that they may enter Paradise without rendering an account. The authorities differ with regard to this. The third intercession is on behalf of those Muslims who ought to go to

[1] Sūrah XVII, 81.
[2] Sweetman, Vol. 2, p. 213.
[3] Sell, *Faith of Islam*, p. 164.

hell. The fourth for those who are already there. No one but the Prophet can make these intercessions. The fifth intercession is for an increase of rank to those who are in Paradise. The Mutazilites maintained that there would be no intercession for Muslims guilty of great sins . . . the orthodox bring in reply to this Hadís-i-Sahíh: "The Prophet said: 'My intercession is for the men of my following who have committed great sins.' "[1]

Koelle says that Tradition declares that 'The dignity has been conferred on Muhammad of acting as Intercessor on the day of resurrection and that he will intercede for seven different categories of people:

> For those who have fled for refuge to Muhammad.
> For those who find their way to Paradise without an account.
> For those deserving punishment.
> For those believers who go to Hell but for whom he intercedes.
> For some already in Paradise that they may receive a higher place.
> For some unbelievers that they may receive lighter punishment.
> For those who die in Medina.'[2]

It is obviously in accordance with this general view in Tradition that among the names and titles commonly given to the Prophet in popular books of devotion are—

'The Intercessor', 'The Pardoner', and 'The Mediator'.[3]

So also, M. Gaudefroy-Demombynes, in describing current Muslim belief and practice, says: 'Then man

---
[1] Sell: *The Faith of Islam*, pp. 169-170.
[2] Koelle, op. cit., p. 427.
[3] Zwemer, op. cit., p. 158.

will appear before Allāh who will cause his acts to be weighed in the balance ... after the final account has been established. The faces of the faithful will be white; those who have denied the faith will have black faces, It is at this moment that the Prophet will intervene. whose intercession in favour of the Muslim community will be accepted by Allāh.'[1]

Here then, is clear evidence that in the early Traditions and in popular Islam up to the present day there is a firm conviction that Muhammad will be the Intercessor in the Day of Judgement. Sweetman suggests that this belief has grown up 'to offset the depressing effect of the doctrine of qadar.[2] It provides a last hope to uneasy minds.'[3] This may well be the true explanation of a development which appears to stand in almost complete contradiction to the teaching of the Prophet recorded in the Qur'an. Sweetman goes on to suggest further, that it brings in an 'alien doctrine' of a saviour through the very pressure of sinful human need. Whether in fact, however, it represents an 'alien doctrine' is a matter of much more uncertainty. We have already noticed that the Qur'an shows a distinct tendency to ascribe to Muhammad powers which are at times more suggestive of a supernatural than a purely human Messenger of God—one who holds direct communion with Gabriel and receives Allāh's revelation; who is taken up to heaven to enjoy intimate and personal communion with God Himself; one who can perform miracles as a proof of the truth of his mission. And we have seen also how in the Traditions, within a comparatively short period of the death of Muhammad, such supernatural aspects of his life and work were developed and magnified. It is against

[1] *Muslim Institutions*, p. 53. Lond. 1950.
[2] 'qadar' is the doctrine of divine pre-destination to good or evil.
[3] Op. cit., Vol. 2, p. 213.

this background that the belief in Muhammad as Intercessor must be viewed, and it then appears, not so much as an alien doctrine, as a logical extension of his other supernatural powers and functions. Prophet, Friend of Allāh, Wonder-worker, Intercessor—these interpretations of the Prophet's person all form distinguishable but closely-related aspects of a figure who became the object of a steadily increasing veneration on the part of the Muslim communities.

THIRTEEN

THE APOTHEOSIS OF THE PROPHET

In view of the facts which have been brought together in the preceding pages from the various sections of the sacred books of Islam, it is apparent that the Prophet came to be regarded as a supernatural figure and that he is so regarded by a very large number of Muslims today. This conclusion is supported, moreover, by scholars whose high reputations in the field of Islamic studies give great weight to their views.

Thus, Dr. Koelle, whose book *Mohammed and Mohammedanism* was published in 1889 and has already been referred to here on numerous occasions, has demonstrated in great detail how the Muslim Traditionists attribute to Muhammad a supernatural character which is comparable with that attributed by the writers of the New Testament to Jesus Christ.

Professor Margoliouth, in his book, *Mohammed and the Rise of Islam*, published in 1906, says:

'At Yathrib the Prophet inherited all the devotion and adulation which had hitherto been bestowed on the idols; and though he never permitted the word worship to be used of the ceremonies of which he was the object, he ere long became hedged in with a state which differed little from that which surrounded a god. Enthusiastic converts habitually struggled for the honour of washing in the water which the Prophet had used for his ablution, and then drinking it up. Ere long he took to bottling up the precious liquid and sending it, after the style of the relics of the saints, to new adherents. When he employed the services of a barber, the Moslems crowded round, and even scrambled for the hair, and nail-parings, which they preserved as charms and relics. The ease of approach which had characterised the old Bedouin chiefs was soon prohibited, and a divine revelation forbade the Moslems to address the Prophet as they addressed each other. At one time he commanded his followers to make an offering to the poor before they addressed him, but this had to be rescinded. He made a rule to enter no house of Medinah with one exception save his own, and perhaps broke it only when it was necessary for him to administer the last consolations to the dying; but after a time it became a custom to bring the dying or dead to him.'[1]

Professor Guillaume, in his book already referred to, *The Traditions of Islam*, published in 1924, says that he has included in the book translations of a few ḥadīth to supplement the work already done by others and 'to show particularly how, with the passing of the years, the fallible human figure of Muhammad has faded into oblivion'.[2]

Richard Bell, in *The Origin of Islam in its Christian Environment*, published in 1926, declares:

'Thus we see, even in the first two centuries, the biography of Muhammad being decked out with all kinds of miraculous and legendary stories which are familiar in the case of the Christian saints and Jewish rabbis . . . These things opened the way for that religious veneration of the Prophet . . . which is so characteristic of, and such a strength to, popular Islam.'[3]

Professor H. A. R. Gibb, in his *Mohammedanism*, published in 1949, refers to the idea of the supernatural character of the Prophet as having special significance in Shī'a and in early Ṣūfī thought:

[1] p. 216.   [2] p. 150.   [3] p. 200.

'The doctrine of the Divine Light and the sinlessness of the Imām was taken over and applied, not to Ali himself but to Ali's master, the Prophet Mohammed, and in conjunction with other causes supplied the basis for an enthusiastic veneration of the Prophet, which has ever been one of the strongest spiritual influences in Sunni Islam.'

In a further significant passage he speaks of another 'graft' on to the stem of Islam, namely 'the evolution of the doctrine of the person of Mohammed'. He says that the Shī'a influences mentioned above helped forward this development but alongside these there were superimposed upon the natural reverence of the believer for the person of the Prophet several of the Christian ideas of the person of Jesus. 'In early Muslim mysticism outside Arabia Jesus still occupies a place alongside and little if at all inferior to Mohammed, but gradually the figure of Mohammed transcends the other, until at the end of the 3rd century we find in the words of the great mystic al-Hallāj a hymn to the Prophet in which Christian and Gnostic images are fused into a triumphant synthesis:

' All the Lights of the Prophets proceeded from his Light; he was before all, his name the first in the Book of Fate; he was known before all things and all being, and will endure after the end of all. By his guidance have all eyes attained to sight. . . . All knowledge is a drop from his ocean, all wisdom a handful from his stream, all times an hour from his life.'

'Here,' Gibb concludes, 'and not in the abstractions of the theologians, is the true spirit of popular Islam, and to this Arabia contributed nothing but the historical existence of Mohammed.'[1]

Probably, however, the fullest and most categorical

[1] pp. 125-126 and 130-131.

statement of opinion is to be found in Dr. Zwemer's book which bears the striking title *The Moslem Christ*, published in 1912. Chapter VII of this book is headed 'Jesus Christ Supplanted by Mohammed', and in it Dr. Zwemer shows how popular Islam, based upon Tradition, plainly regards the Prophet as imbued with divine qualities and characteristics. He shows that the two hundred and one titles of honour given to the Prophet 'proclaim his apotheosis' and says that many of them are also applied by Muslims themselves to Allāh, as well as to the Prophet. Among them are the following:

The Forgiver, The Perfect, The Answerer of Prayer, The Interceder, The Mediator, Righteousness, The Justifier, The Holy One, Holy Spirit, Spirit of Truth, The Source of Truth, The Pardoner of Sins.

He also declares that one Tradition goes so far as to say:

'No man in whatsoever condition he is can resemble God so much as thou dost. But if there could be an image to represent God as He is, it could be no other than thyself.'

Regarding all this from the standpoint of the Christian apologist, Dr. Zwemer declares:

'The sin and guilt of the Mohammedan world is that they give Christ's glory to another, *and that for all practical purposes Mohammed himself is the Moslem Christ.*'[1]

[1] See pp. 157-160.

PART III
THE CHRIST

FOURTEEN

THE SOURCES

The outlines of the tradition of the birth, life and death of Jesus are well known. The year of his birth is now supposed to have been 4 B.C. rather than A.D. 1. He is said by St. Luke to have been 'about thirty years of age' at the time when his public ministry began, and the ministry is usually thought to have lasted for three years, so that the year A.D. 29 may, if these two assumptions are correct, be regarded as the approximate year of his death. He was born into the family of Joseph, a carpenter of the city of Nazareth in Galilee; became an itinerant preacher in Judaea and Galilee, whose followers regarded him as the promised Messiah; and was put to death by the religious leaders of his people, whose bitter hostility he had aroused.

It is, of course, from the New Testament that virtually all our knowledge of Jesus is derived. One of the earliest references to him in contemporary non-Christian works seems to be that of Josephus: writing towards the end of the 1st century he mentions his execution in a few lines.[1] In the 'Annales' of Tacitus it is said that 'Christus, from whom the name (Christians) had its origin, suffered the extreme penalty during the reign of Tiberius at the hands of one of our procurators, Pontius Pilate.' This was written about the year 115. Pliny, the governor of Bithynia, had written to the Emperor Trajan about three years earlier asking for guidance in dealing with the Christians in his province, but he makes no reference to Christ himself.

[1] Antiquities XVIII, III, §3: the passage has been considered spurious by some scholars.

Among the books of the New Testament, the four Gospels, of course, represent the chief source of information about the birth, life and death of Jesus. It is now generally agreed that the Gospel of St. Mark is the earliest and was probably written about the year A.D. 65. It was used as the basis of the Gospels of St. Matthew and St. Luke, the date of the former being generally taken to be *c*. A.D. 80-85 and of the latter *c*. A.D. 75-85. The Gospel of St. John, which is even more deliberately didactic in its approach than the three Synoptic Gospels, is generally assumed to be the latest of the four, and to belong to the period of the end of the first century or even the beginning of the second.

Certain additional facts are to be gathered from other parts of the New Testament, especially the Epistles of St. Paul, St. John and the Epistle to the Hebrews. St. Paul's Epistles seem to have been written before the year A.D. 64, when he is believed to have died in the great persecution of Nero at Rome. The Epistles of St. John appear to belong to the same period as the Gospel, and the Epistle to the Hebrews seems to have been written at some time between the years A.D. 70 and 85.

It will therefore be obvious at once that we are dealing with accounts of and references to the life of Christ which all belong to a period removed by about thirty-five years at least and in some cases possibly as much as eighty years, from the traditional date of his death. The fact that such a comparatively long period elapsed before written records of the ministry were compiled is accounted for by the widespread belief among the first generation of Christians that Christ would return in triumph during their life-time and usher in the end of the age. Thus, even had it occurred to these first generation Christians, the idea of handing on a written record of Jesus' life and teaching would have seemed pointless. It was only as a result of the delay in the occurrence of the second advent of Christ and because of the death of numbers of the first-generation converts that the need for such records as the Gospels gradually came to be appreciated.

The intervening period—the period of 'the oral tradition'—has occupied the close attention of New Testament scholars within recent times. Some of them have argued that during this period the traditions of the birth, life, teaching and death of Jesus gradually assumed a shape or shapes which were much more the result of the influence of the preaching, and increasingly organised, Church and were much less simple, historical records of a factual kind. In Germany in particular, the group of scholars who have come to be known as the 'Form Critics' and of whom one of the best-known is Dr. Martin Dibelius, have carried this argument to considerable lengths. Thus Dr. Dibelius holds that the material out of which the Evangelists compiled their written records of the ministry had already assumed certain definite 'Forms' when it came into their hands, and that these 'Forms' can be recognised and understood by reference to certain laws of sacred biography which are not by any means confined to the record of the Christian tradition.[1]

Few English scholars have been disposed to go as far as Dr. Dibelius goes in assessing the significance of the Form Critical method, though it is apparent that some conclusions, at any rate, of this method cannot be ignored. Probably Dr. Vincent Taylor is one of the foremost of the more moderate English exponents of Form Criticism and his views have been set out in his work, *The Formation of the Gospel Tradition*.[2] In general it would seem true to say that as a result of the work of the Form Critics most

[1] See *From Tradition to Gospel*. Trans. B. L. Wolf, Lond. 1934.
[2] Lond. 1933. For more cautious views still, see Tasker, *The Nature and Purpose of the Gospels*, Lond. 1944, and Dodd, *The Apostolic Teaching and its Development*, Lond. 1936.

scholars of the New Testament are now disposed to recognise the fact that the Gospels owe part at least of their points of view about the person and ministry of Jesus and of their arrangement of the material, more to the mind and needs of the preaching Church and less to the desire for a simple, objective, historical record of his life and teaching.

FIFTEEN

THE PRE-EXISTENCE, CONCEPTION AND BIRTH OF THE CHRIST

The belief in Christ's pre-existence is met with first in St. Paul's writings. In the Epistle to the Philippians he exhorts the Christians at Philippi:

'Have this mind in you, which was also in Christ Jesus: who, being in the form of God, counted it not a prize to be on an equality with God, but emptied himself, taking the form of a servant, being made in the likeness of men; and being found in fashion as a man, he humbled himself, becoming obedient even unto death, yea, the death of the cross. Wherefore also God highly exalted him, and gave unto him the name which is above every name that in the name of Jesus every knee should bow, of things in heaven and things on earth and things under the earth, and that every tongue should confess that Jesus Christ is Lord, to the glory of God the Father.'[1]

The word 'form' here ($\mu o \rho \phi \acute{\eta}$) means the 'essential shape or character' and the whole passage suggests that the Christ was from the beginning divine.

A second even plainer assertion of Christ's pre-existence occurs in the opening verses of the Epistle to the Hebrews, where the author says that God 'Hath at the end of these days spoken unto us in his Son, whom he appointed heir of all things, through whom also he made the worlds; who being the effulgence of his glory, and the very image of his substance, and upholding all things by the word of his power, when he had made purification of sins, sat down on the right hand of the majesty on

[1] Phil. ii. 5-11.

high; having become by so much better than the angels, as he hath inherited a more excellent name than they.'[1] Here again, it is apparent that in this writer's view, Christ appears, as Dr. Quick puts it, 'on the divine side of the differentiating line' (i.e. between creator and creature) and that as the one through whom God made the worlds, he pre-existed with God from the beginning.

The three synoptic gospels do not refer to Christ's pre-existence but the Fourth Gospel does. In the most moving prologue in chapter one, it is said:

'In the beginning was the Word (λόγος) and the Word was with God and the Word was God. The same was in the beginning with God. All things were made by him; and without him was not anything made that hath been made. In him was life and the life was the light of men. And the light shineth in the darkness; and the darkness apprehended it not. ... And the Word became flesh, and dwelt among us.'[2]

This solemn declaration, though not referred to subsequently in the body of the Gospel in the same metaphorical form, is in complete harmony with the whole point of view of the Gospel, in which the Christ is set forth pre-eminently as the 'true light' of God shining in the darkness that pervades the *cosmos*. The human life of Christ is a real life but it is ultimately the means by which the eternal 'Word' of God is set forth to men. The Christ therefore becomes incarnate, sets forth the truth to men, attested by 'signs' and passes to the Cross and finally to the resurrection, all in accordance with a pre-ordained plan.

It is in the total setting of the christological thought of the Gospel and Epistles of St. John therefore, that the doctrine of Christ's pre-existence assumes the most

[1] Heb. i. 2-4.   [2] John i. 1-5 and 14.

natural place—a more natural place than it does in either St. Paul or the Epistle to the Hebrews. In St. Paul's thought and in that of Hebrews, the emphasis is primarily upon the fact of Christ's humanity. St. Paul regards him as the one perfect human representative of the Jewish race, through whom the promises made to 'the fathers' are fulfilled. It is from the thought of what God has wrought for man's redemption in the Christ that he passes to the thought of Christ's divinity and introduces the idea of his pre-existence, thus taking Christ's Sonship back into the past.[1] The writer of the Epistle to the Hebrews similarly emphasises the humanity of Christ: he is the 'great high priest' who has dedicated by his blood 'a new and living way' for man. Here again, from the thought of all that is involved in this great act of redemption, he passes to the thought of the divinity of the redeemer who is in fact the pre-existent 'Son of God'.

It has been argued that the 'Logos' doctrine in the Prologue of St. John's Gospel presents affinities with the Logos doctrine of Philo, the Jewish philosopher of the first century, with the World—Reason of Stoicism, and with the use of the term 'Memra' or 'Word' in Jewish Targums as a periphrastic expression to avoid the direct use of the Divine Name in referring to God. It is not improbable that in a Gospel which seems to have emanated from and been written particularly for Christians in Asia Minor, some attempt should have been made to present Christ in terms already reasonably familiar in contemporary Hellenistic thought: indeed, this is obviously one of the main purposes in the mind

[1] In his Bampton Lectures called 'The New Testament Doctrine of the Christ,' London 1926, Dr. Rawlinson recognises the 'development' involved in the New Testament interpretation of the person of Christ and says that St. Paul 'introduces' the idea of His pre-existence, suggesting that the idea itself was derived from the conception of Christ as the 'Heavenly Man' of apocalyptic literature. See the whole passage on p. 225.

of the writer throughout the Gospel. On the other hand, some scholars are disinclined to accept such a view: thus Dr. Rawlinson says that it 'appears highly improbable' that 'the Evangelist was in any way directly dependent upon the speculations of Philo or upon any alternative form of Hellenistic religious philosophy.' He argues that the writer has in fact adopted the term 'Logos' from current usage at Ephesus in order to express by its means a 'Wisdom' Christology which is essentially Hebraic.[1]

However, the actual significance of the belief in the pre-existence of Christ is plain, namely that it depicts his earthly advent and ministry in the setting of its eternal significance. The Christ who was born in Bethlehem as man had in fact 'emptied himself, taking the form of a servant, being made in the likeness of men.'

This same motive obviously underlies also the traditional stories of the Virgin Birth of Jesus, alluded to only in the Gospels of St. Matthew and St. Luke. The version of St. Matthew is as follows:

'Now the birth of Jesus Christ was on this wise: When his mother Mary had been betrothed to Joseph, before they came together she was found with child of the Holy Ghost. And Joseph, her husband, being a righteous man, and not willing to make her a public example, was minded to put her away privily. But when he thought on these things, behold, an angel of the Lord appeared to him in a dream, saying, Joseph, thou son of David, fear not to take unto thee Mary thy wife: for that which is conceived in her is of the Holy Ghost. And she shall bring forth a son; and thou shalt call his name Jesus; for it is he that shall save his people from their sins. Now all this is come to pass that it might be fulfilled which was spoken by the Lord through the prophet, saying Behold, the

---

[1] Op. cit., p. 210.

virgin shall be with child, and shall bring forth a son, and they shall call his name Immanuel; which is, being interpreted, God with us. And Joseph arose from his sleep, and did as the angel of the Lord commanded him, and took unto him his wife and knew her not till she had brought forth a son: and he called his name Jesus.'[1]

In St. Luke's story of the birth an angel appears to Mary: indeed, the reader's attention is focused throughout upon the experiences, not of Joseph, but of Mary:

'Now in the sixth month the angel Gabriel was sent from God until a city of Galilee, named Nazareth, to a virgin betrothed to a man whose name was Joseph, of the house of David and the virgin's name was Mary. And he came in unto her and said, Hail, thou that art highly favoured, the Lord is with thee. But she was greatly troubled at the saying, and cast in her mind what manner of salutation this might be. And the angel said unto her, Fear not, Mary: for thou hast found favour with God. And, behold, thou shalt conceive in thy womb, and bring forth a son, and shalt call his name Jesus. He shall be great and shall be called the Son of the Most High; and the Lord God shall give unto him the throne of his father David, and he shall reign over the house of Jacob for ever; and of his kingdom there shall be no end. And Mary said unto the angel, How shall this be, seeing I know not a man? And the angel answered and said unto her, The Holy Ghost shall come upon thee, and the power of the Most High shall overshadow thee; wherefore also that which is to be born shall be called holy, Son of God. And, behold, Elisabeth thy kinswoman she also hath conceived a son in her old age: and this is the sixth month with her that was called barren. For no word from God shall be void of power. And Mary said,

[1] S. Matt. i. 18-25.

Behold, the handmaid of the Lord; be it unto me according to thy word. And the angel departed from her.'[1]

'And it came to pass, while they were there, the days were fulfilled that she should be delivered. And she brought forth her firstborn son; and she wrapped him in swaddling clothes and laid him in a manger, because there was no room for them in the inn.'[2]

So much has been written on the subject of the Virgin Birth that it is impossible, nor is it necessary here, to attempt to discuss it fully. The following significant facts, however, are worth bearing in mind at this point.

(1) The tradition is found in each case in a Gospel which is acknowledged to have been written between A.D. 75 and 85, and in those sections of them which are not parts of the Marcan traditions. This fact and the silence of St. Paul on the subject would seem to suggest that the tradition is not among the earliest traditions of the life of Jesus.

(2) The allusion in St. Matthew to the passage from Isaiah vii. 14, which some of the early Christians evidently used mistakenly as a support for the belief, suggests that possibly the tradition gained ground by being interpreted as further evidence of the fulfilment of Old Testament prophecy. It must be remembered that such 'fulfilment' was eagerly searched out by the communities of early Jewish Christians.

(3) In modern discussion of the problems raised by the tradition it is frequently asserted that the ultimate criterion for accepting or rejecting the belief is in fact doctrinal and not its justification on grounds of historical proof. Perhaps the clearest statement of this position is that made in the 'Report on Doctrine in the Church of England,' which says:

[1] Luke i. 26-38. [2] Luke ii. 6-7.

'The main grounds on which the doctrine is valued are the following. It is a safeguard of the Christian conviction that in the birth of Jesus we have, not simply the birth of a new individual of the human species, but the advent of One who "for us men and for our salvation came down from heaven." It is congruous with the belief that in the Person of Christ humanity made a fresh beginning. It coheres with the supernatural element in the life of Christ, indicating a unique inauguration of that unique life. It gives expression to the idea of the response of the human race to God's purpose through the obedience and faith of the Blessed Virgin Mary.

'Many of us hold, accordingly, that belief in the Word made flesh is integrally bound up with belief in the Virgin Birth, and that this will increasingly be recognised.'[1]

This passage, interestingly enough, reflects that motive which was probably, in fact, also the original one behind the development of the tradition of the miraculous birth of Christ, namely the desire to emphasise the great significance of the advent of one who was the eternal 'Son of God'. In his Schweich Lectures for 1942, the late Dr. W. L. Knox pointed out that Judaism, at about the beginning of the Christian era, abounded in stories of miraculous births of such great figures as Noah, Abraham, Isaac, Moses, Samuel and Samson, and that the 'motif' of a miraculous birth was in no way strange to Jewish thought. That similar stories abounded also in the Hellenistic world of the first century A.D. is well known. He came to the conclusion that it is more likely that the story of the virgin birth has been influenced by the folk-lore of Judaism rather than by that of the Greek world, and suggested that the underlying motive behind

[1] p. 82. See also *The Historical Evidence for the Virgin Birth*, by Vincent Taylor, pp. 130 ff: Oxf. 1920.

such stories is the 'belief that a miraculous birth was in some way suitable for anyone whose greatness made him the equal of the heroes of antiquity.'[1]

The same two Gospels which contain the traditional account of the virgin birth of Christ also connect with the birth a number of marvellous events, thus heightening yet further the supernatural significance of his advent into the world. St. Matthew contains the story of the visit of the Magi, guided by a star to Jerusalem, and from thence to Bethlehem with the advice of the 'chief priests and scribes of the people.' An 'angel of the Lord' appears in a dream to Joseph and warns him to take the young child into Egypt to avoid the wrath of Herod, and so yet another Old Testament prophecy is fulfilled, for 'it was spoken by the Lord through the prophet, saying, Out of Egypt did I call my son.' A second appearance of an angel heralds the return of the family from Egypt to Galilee.[2]

St. Luke's Gospel contains the stories of the appearance of the angel to the shepherds which led to their visit to Bethlehem and their discovery of the infant Jesus; and of the prophecies of Simeon and of 'Anna, a prophetess', on the occasion of the presentation of the infant Christ in the Temple in Jerusalem.[3]

All these stories are so well known that it is unnecessary to print them here in full, but certain points about them may be noted. The idea of the appearance of astronomical portents as attesting some outstanding event in human affairs is also found outside Christian tradition. In Classical literature particularly it occurs more than once: Virgil in the Aeneid speaks of a star guiding Aeneas to the future site of Rome; Suetonius suggests that a star foretold the birth of Augustus; Cicero recounts

---

[1] *Some Hellenistic Elements in Primitive Christianity*, pp. 22-25, Lond. 1944.
[2] Matt. ii.   [3] Luke ii. 8-20 and 22-39.

a story of how Asiatic Magi saw a bright star burning in the night in which Alexander the Great had been born.[1] There is evidence also, that similar legends abounded in the Jewish Midrashic literature of the period, in some cases closely parallel in details to this Matthaen legend.[2] It seems possible that St. Matthew's version is derived partly from these Jewish and partly also from Persian sources. Discussion has taken place about the possibility of an actual historical phenomenon of an astronomical character as the basis of the story, but there is no real evidence for assuming such an occurrence and it is more likely that the real origin of the legend is, as suggested above, other similar legends.

While the main motive behind this legend in St. Matthew's Gospel is clear, namely to imbue the birth of the Christ with fitting supernatural significance, it is possible that the author of the Gospel was also concerned with a secondary motive, namely to stress the conflict between the true 'king of Jerusalem' and the earthly king—a symbol of the conflict between the heavenly and the earthly 'kingdom' which is a recurring theme of the Gospel.

[1] Aeneid II, 694; Tacitus, Hist. V. 12; Suetonius, Augustus, 94; Cicero, de Div. 247 etc.
[2] See Box, *The Virgin Birth of Jesus*, p. 19; Lond. 1916.

SIXTEEN

THE CALL

The immediate preludes to the beginning of Christ's public ministry are traditionally said to have been his baptism by John Baptist and the temptation in the wilderness. The New Testament versions of both traditions make it clear that in the mind of the early Church these incidents are significant as revealing that the divine seal was, from the start, set upon the ministry.

St. Mark's account of the baptism is as follows: 'And it came to pass in those days that Jesus came from Nazareth of Galilee, and was baptized of John in the Jordan. And straightway coming up out of the water, he saw the heavens rent asunder, and the Spirit as a dove descending upon him: and a voice came out of the heavens, Thou art my beloved Son, in thee I am well pleased.'[1]

St. Matthew's version is fuller and is largely concerned to explain away a difficulty experienced by some of the early Christians in accepting the story of the baptism, namely the incongruity of the need for the baptism of one who was regarded as sinless. Jesus is therefore made to explain that for him baptism is an annointing of the Servant of Jehovah for his office, in accordance with the prophecy of Is. lxi. 1.[2]

St. Luke's version is very brief and appears to put all the emphasis upon the fact of the divine voice.[3]

All three accounts agree in asserting that immediately after the act of baptism, the 'Spirit' descended upon Jesus 'as a dove' and that a voice came out of the heavens saying 'Thou art my beloved Son; in thee I am well

[1] Mark i. 9-11.   [2] Matt. iii. 13-17.   [3] Luke iii. 21-22.

pleased.' St. John's Gospel contains no direct account of the baptism but makes John Baptist declare:

'And John bare witness, saying, I have beheld the Spirit descending as a dove out of heaven; and it abode upon him. And I knew him not: but he that sent me to baptize with water, he said unto me, Upon whomsoever thou shalt see the Spirit descending, and abiding upon him, the same is he that baptizeth with the Holy Spirit. And I have seen, and have borne witness that this is the Son of God.'[1]

Thus the tradition of the heavenly voice at the baptism is mentioned in all four Gospels and it seems legitimate to conclude from this fact that it was this particular aspect of the tradition which came to be regarded by the early Christians as especially significant, because it provided striking evidence to them of the supernatural character of Christ's person and message.[2]

The Story of the temptation of Christ by 'Satan' in the wilderness during forty days following the baptism, is told in detail by St. Matthew and St. Luke, who appear to be following the tradition embodied in the source known to New Testament scholars as 'Q'. St. Mark's reference to the temptation, however, is brief; it consists of only two verses and contains none of the detail given in the other two Synoptic Gospels. It will be sufficient here to reproduce St. Luke's version:

'And Jesus, full of the Holy Spirit, returned from Jordan, and was led by the Spirit in the wilderness during

---

[1] John i. 32-34.
[2] This is evidently also the view of Dr. Blunt in his 'Clarendon' commentary on St. Mark. He says: 'The story of the voice from heaven at the baptism must not be taken literally here. ... It is a piece of what the Rabbis called "midrash" ... we may take the detail as merely expressing the sense of divine assurance and authority, which henceforth came on Jesus.', p. 140; Lond. 1929.

forty days, being tempted of the devil. And he did eat nothing in those days: and when they were completed, he hungered. And the devil said unto him, If thou art the Son of God, command this stone that it become bread. And Jesus answered unto him, It is written, Man shall not live by bread alone. And he led him up, and shewed him all the kingdoms of the world in a moment of time. And the devil said unto him, To thee will I give all this authority, and the glory of them: for it hath been delivered unto me: and to whomsoever I will I give it. If thou therefore wilt worship before me, it shall all be thine. And Jesus answered and said unto him, It is written, Thou shalt worship the Lord thy God, and him only shalt thou serve. And he led him to Jerusalem, and set him on the pinnacle of the temple, and said unto him, If thou art the Son of God, cast thyself down from hence: for it is written,

He shall give his angels charge concerning thee, to guard thee: and On their hands they shall bear thee up, Lest haply thou dash thy foot against a stone. And Jesus answering said unto him, It is said, Thou shalt not tempt the Lord thy God. And when the devil had completed every temptation, he departed from him for a season.'[1]

For all its brevity, however, St. Mark's reference to the temptation says that after it was all over, 'angels ministered unto him': St. Matthew also adds the same words, and they are obviously significant as indicating one point of view from which the early Church regarded this tradition. While it is clear that the main motive for including the story was to show that current Jewish conceptions of the character of the Messiah and his work

---

[1] Luke iv. 1-12; cf. Matt. iv. 1-11; Mark i. 12-13. St. John, understandably, makes no reference to the tradition.

were in fact mistaken, it is also plain that part of its value lay in the manner in which it depicted the beginnings of the ministry in a supernatural light. The powers of evil, symbolised here by the 'devil', the 'adversary' of mankind, are seen ranged against the saviour of men, in an attempt to divert him from the path of the divine purpose. The moving reference to angels succouring the victorious Christ suggests still further the idea of the Divine approval and support and so helps to make it abundantly clear that the ministry which is to follow is a revelation of the Divine Will and Purpose.

SEVENTEEN

THE MINISTRY

(a) *The Transfiguration.*

As the story of the heavenly voice which spoke at the baptism attested the supernatural character of the ministry at its inception, so the story of the Transfiguration provides a second and similar supernatural testimony as the ministry progresses. The story of the Transfiguration occurs in all three Synoptic Gospels: obviously St. Mark is here being followed by St. Matthew and St. Luke, and the slight differences between the three accounts are in details only. It will therefore be sufficient if St. Mark's account is quoted here:

'And after six days Jesus taketh with him Peter, and James, and John, and bringeth them up into a high mountain apart by themselves: and he was transfigured before them: and his garments became glistering, exceeding white; so as no fuller on earth can whiten them. And there appeared unto them Elijah with Moses: and they were talking with Jesus. And Peter answereth and saith to Jesus, Rabbi, it is good for us to be here: and let us make three tabernacles: one for thee, and one for Moses, and one for Elijah. For he wist not what to answer; for they became sore afraid. And there came a cloud overshadowing them: and there came a voice out of the cloud, This is my beloved Son: hear ye him. And suddenly looking round about, they saw no one any more, save Jesus only with themselves.'[1]

There is a close and striking resemblance between

---
[1] Mark ix. 2-8; cf. Matt. xvii. 1-8; Luke ix. 28-36.

the 'voice out of the cloud' here and the voice heard at the baptism. The formulae used in both cases are so evidently similar that we must assume that both traditions have here been influenced by the Rabbinical conception of the 'bath kol' or 'daughter of the voice'. Among the numerous poetical ideas to be found in the Rabbinical writings we find that of the 'voice from heaven' (called 'bath kol'); references to it usually, as here and in the tradition of the baptism, took the form of a quotation partly from Ps. ii. 7 and partly from Is. xlii. 1.

Obviously this testimony of the heavenly voice represents the climax of the story as it is set forth here in tradition: it was clearly taken by the early Church as yet further evidence of the Divine character of and of the Divine seal set upon Christ's ministry. Dr. K. E. Kirk has underlined this point in his book *The Vision of God*. He says that the Church had from the beginning fixed upon the Transfiguration as the central moment of Christ's earthly life and that it was a vivid reminder that 'the whole Gospel from beginning to end must be read and regarded as one great vision of God in Christ, divinity breaking through the humanity of Jesus.'[1]

(b) *The Miracles*.

The miracles of Christ referred to in the canonical records of his ministry are so numerous and so well known that it does not seem either reasonable or necessary to quote them here in full; it is sufficient if they are listed.

At once, however, we find ourselves faced with the difficulty of deciding upon a satisfactory classification of them. Two of the most recent books dealing with the miracles of Christ have included quite different attempts on the part of their authors at such a classification.

---

[1] pp. 97-101: Abridged Edn.; Lond. 1934.

Professor Alan Richardson's book, *The Miracle Stories of the Gospels*, first published in 1941, aims at presenting the miracle-stories as just as truly a part of the preaching of the early Church as the parables, or the more directly didactic aspects of the Gospels. In accordance with this general aim, the miracle-stories are discussed under such heads as 'Jesus as Healer and Bringer of Forgiveness', 'Christ as the Lord of Wind and Waves'; etc.[1] On the other hand Prof. Lewis's *Miracles*, published in 1947, suggests that the miracles can be classified in two ways. The first system yields six categories—Miracles of (1) Fertility, (2) of Healing, (3) of Destruction, (4) of Dominion over the Inorganic, (5) of Reversal, and (6) of Perfecting or Glorification. These may, however, all be grouped under two headings—(1) Miracles of the Old Creation, and (2) Miracles of the New Creation.[2]

Though interesting and suggestive in their respective contexts, neither of these classifications is quite suitable for the mainly descriptive and comparative standpoint which is our present concern. It therefore seems better to fall back on an obvious and simpler principle of classification, even if it may in certain cases suffer from the slight disadvantage of being less precise than some might wish. Apart from the traditions of great miraculous events associated with the person of Christ Himself—the Incarnation, the Virgin Birth, the Temptation, the Transfiguration, and the Resurrection and the Ascension—all of which will here have been afforded special and separate consideration, it is possible to group the traditions of the miracles of the ministry under three main heads:

(1) Nature Miracles,
(2) Miracles of healing or resurrection,
(3) The Foretelling of future events.

[1] See esp. Chs. IV and V.   [2] See Chs. XV and XVI.

(1) *Nature Miracles.*
   The turning of water into wine (John)
   The miraculous draught of fishes (Luke)
   The stilling of the storm (Syns.)
   The feeding of the multitudes (5,000 and 4,000) (Syns. and John)
   The walking upon the water (Matt., Mark, John)
   The provision of the tribute-money (Matt., Mark)
   The withering of the fig tree (Matt., Mark).

(2) *Miracles of Healing or Resurrection.*
   The healing of a nobleman's son (John)
   The healing of a demoniac (Mark, Luke)
   The healing of Peter's mother-in-law and others (Syns.)
   The healing of a leper in Galilee (Syns.)
   The healing of the paralytic in Capernaum (Syns.)
   The healing of an infirm man in the Pool of Bethesda (John)
   The healing of the withered hand (Syns.)
   The healing of the centurion's servant (Matt. and Luke)
   The raising of the widow's son (Luke)
   The healing of a demoniac in Galilee (Syns.)
   The healing of two demoniacs at Gadara (Syns.)
   The raising of Jairus' daughter (Syns.)
   The healing of two blind men (Matt.)
   The casting out of a dumb spirit (Matt.)
   The healing of the daughter of a Syro-Phoenician woman (Matt. and Mark)
   The healing of a deaf and dumb man and others near Decapolis (Matt. and Mark)
   The healing of a blind man at Bethsaida (Mark)
   The healing of a demoniac near Caesarea Philippi (Syns.)

The healing of ten lepers (Luke)
The healing of a man born blind (John)
The raising of Lazarus (John)
The healing of an infirm woman (Luke)
The healing of two blind men near Jericho (Syns.)
The healing of the soldier's ear (Luke).

(3) *The Foretelling of Future Events.*
First foretelling of his death and resurrection in Galilee (Syns.)
Second foretelling of his death and resurrection in Galilee (Syns.)
Prophecy in Peraea of his second advent (Luke)
Third foretelling of his death and resurrection, in Peraea (Syns.)
Destruction of the Temple (Syns.)
Various references to the second advent, on the Mount of Olives (Syns.)
The Fall of Peter (Syns. and John)
The coming of the Holy Spirit (John)
The persecution to come (John).

The New Testament writers speak of the miracles of Christ as 'powers' ($\delta\upsilon\nu\acute{\alpha}\mu\epsilon\iota\varsigma$), as 'signs' ($\sigma\eta\mu\epsilon\hat{\iota}\alpha$) and as 'wonders' ($\tau\acute{\epsilon}\rho\alpha\tau\alpha$) in the phrase 'signs and wonders'. It has sometimes been suggested that the Fourth Gospel was concerned in a special sense with these 'signs' as manifestations on the temporal plane of the incarnate Son of God and hardly at all with the miracles as actual historical events. This is to some extent true, in that the 'historicity' of the miracles mentioned in St. John is even more clearly of secondary importance from the standpoint of this Gospel than it is in the case of the Synoptic Gospels.[1] At the same time it is clear that

---
[1] See Richardson, op. cit., pp. 116 ff.

behind the Synoptic traditions of the miracles also is to be discerned a clear didactic motive; the stories of miracles are used as vehicles by means of which instruction and exhortation may be conveyed. This is in fact the main theme of Professor Richardson's book already referred to. He says:

'The truth is that . . . the miracles are a part of the Gospel itself; Christ is to the New Testament writers the manifestation of the power of God in the world, and His mighty deeds are the signs of the effectual working of that power.'[1]

Professor Richardson here touches upon the important point which we noticed at the beginning of this section —namely, the nature and the extent of the influence exerted by the preaching Church upon the formation of the written accounts of Christ's birth, life and death. It is, in fact, in connection with the problems raised in an acute form by the accounts of the miracles in the Gospels that Form Criticism has made some of its most radical pronouncements. In general the Form Critical Method, as expounded by scholars like Bultmann and Dibelius, leads to the conclusion that the miracle stories of the Gospels can be reduced to a literary 'form' which is the direct outcome of a desire to set forth a prophet as a 'wonder-worker'. Both Bultmann and Dibelius are impressed by the fact that the miracle stories of the Gospels possess a remarkable resemblance to the Hellenistic miracle narratives. Thus Dibelius calls the miracle story 'Novelle' or 'Tale' and says that in it Jesus is represented purely and simply as the great miracle worker; the interest is concentrated on the thaumaturge when his acts are described; the Tales reveal a lack of devotional motives, and the gradual retreat of any work of Jesus of general value. They bear, he says, close comparison as to

[1] Op. cit., p. 126.

literary style with similar stories in ancient (Greek and Rabbinic) and modern (stories of healings at Lourdes) writings: stories of healing and raising from the dead are common in these non-Christian writings, as are nature-miracles. 'When I characterise this attitude of the Tales, as secular,' he adds, 'I do not mean that the material itself is of non-Christian origin. Yet there is a certain relationship of kind between the Gospel Tales and the non-Christian miracle stories, and thus a certain approximation to the literature of "the world", not, of course, to fine literature, but to popular literature and indeed to the writing of the people. . . By telling such Tales, the pre-eminence of the "Lord Jesus" could be demonstrated and all other rival gods who were worshipped driven from the field.'[1]

Professor Richardson, on the other hand, argues that the stories must be accepted as so essential 'a part of the Gospel itself' that they can be explained away only by rejecting 'the Gospel' of the Evangelists. 'If we accept their Gospel, we accept the history which they record, and we do not find it difficult to believe with them that the *form* of the revelation which God made in Christ included the working of the "signs" which proclaimed to the opened eyes the fulfilment of the age-long hope of the prophets of Israel, the promise that God would visit and redeem His people.'[2] While, however, thus apparently suggesting that the miracle stories must be accepted as an essential part of the whole Christian Gospel, he contrives to allow the possibility of setting aside certain details in the stories. 'It may be true that we cannot state precisely what happened when Jesus encountered a hungry multitude by the lakeside, or a demented outcast among the tombs, yet there is still a *residuum* which faith

---

[1] *From Tradition to Gospel*, pp. 93-96.
[2] Op. cit., p. 126.

can and must affirm, that the power of God was there made manifest to those who witnessed the act of the Lord, after their eyes had been opened.'[1]

The French scholar, Grandmaison, writing from a conservative orthodox standpoint, takes up, in his three-volume work *Jesus Christ*, an even more precise position than does Professor Richardson. He regards the miracle stories which appear in contemporary Greek or Rabbinic or Christian Apocryphal writings as 'childish' in character and says: 'It is far otherwise with the miracles of Jesus: tokens of higher, spiritual, eternal realities, works of light and goodness, they are none the less works of power, and as such inaugurate the Kingdom of God, whose vital representations they are.'[2]

It does, however, seem clear that as they are used by the Evangelists—and therefore presumably as understood by the Churches of the 1st century A.D.—the miracle-stories had come to acquire a symbolic significance for the Church's interpretation of the birth, life and death of Christ which puts them into a category far removed from that of Tales of a 'wonder worker'. The Christ who fed the multitude was the Christ who was regarded as the 'Bread of Life' by the harassed, persecuted Christians of the 1st century for whom even to gather together in worship often meant risking their lives. The Christ who stilled the storm on the Sea of Galilee was He who could quiet and strengthen the hearts of those of His followers who were beginning to feel the Church tossing on the angry sea of Roman persecution. The Christ who could raise the dead was the Christ who could lead his faithful servants to their own ultimate triumph over the grave.

[1] Op. cit., p. 129.
[2] Vol. III, p. 150 in the English Translation, Lond. 1935.

EIGHTEEN

THE DEATH, RESURRECTION AND ASCENSION OF THE CHRIST

The Synoptic Gospels agree in recording that two marvellous happenings occurred as Jesus died: there came 'a darkness over the whole land' from the sixth to the ninth hour, and the Temple veil was rent from top to bottom. St. Matthew's version adds a number of other happenings of a similarly unusual character: an earthquake took place and dead saints came out of their tombs and were seen by people in Jerusalem. St. John's Gospel omits all reference to these stories.

The 'Temple veil' referred to here is probably that which divided the Holy Place from the Holy of Holies. There seems, however, to be a large measure of agreement among New Testament commentators that all the stories of mysterious portents alluded to in this part of the tradition more probably have their origin in the common and fairly widespread belief that earthly events of great significance were accompanied by supernatural portents. Once again, therefore, we see a manifestation of the conviction that the death of a prophet, whose life had been of great significance, could not be allowed to take place without some demonstration of a supernatural kind to set his passing in its supernatural perspective.

Accounts of the resurrection of Christ occur in all four Gospels, and it is alluded to in other parts of the New Testament. It has frequently been pointed out that the various accounts are difficult to reconcile: there is, however, general agreement about the main events, which the tradition describes thus. On the first day of the week, two days after the crucifixion, some of Jesus' followers discovered that the stone had been rolled away from the entrance of the rock tomb in which he had been buried and that the tomb itself was empty. There was at first evident perplexity among the followers of Jesus at this development, but later it gave way to a conviction that he had 'risen from the dead'. This conviction was the result of a number of appearances of Jesus to his followers during the forty days following the first discovery of the empty tomb: there is, however, some disagreement among the New Testament writers about the exact circumstances of these resurrection appearances.

The whole background against which the appearances are set is one of mystery. On the one hand the traditions represent the risen Christ as manifesting a normal physical body, in which the wounds inflicted during the crucifixion are evident, and on the other they lay stress upon the fact that he is not subject to the usual restrictions and limitations of physical existence. Thus he can pass in and out of a locked room; he can disappear mysteriously from mortal sight; and he warns his followers that he must not be touched; yet he is said to have insisted that 'a spirit hath not flesh and bones, as ye behold me having.'[1]

This last quotation is of special significance; it embodies the firm conviction of the early Christians that the resurrection of Jesus was in a different category from that of a mere survival after death. It has often been pointed out that the form in which the Christian tradition of the resurrection of Christ was handed down was Hebraic and not Hellenistic: the Hebrews did not, like the Greeks, believe in the survival of an embodied soul, but, as here, in the revival or resurrection of the whole person, of whom the body was an essential aspect.

---

[1] Luke xxiv. 39.

Many attempts have been made to explain the occurrences which actually lay behind the tradition of the resurrection of Jesus, into details of which it is not necessary to go here. Of the extent, however, to which the followers of Jesus were influenced by their conviction that God had raised up Jesus, there is no doubt at all: indeed it would be reasonable to say that this conviction represents the very core of primitive Christianity. The disciples themselves were sufficiently encouraged and inspired by it to go out and preach in Jerusalem, and the central theme of their message was that Christ 'being delivered up by the determinate counsel and foreknowledge of God, ye by the hand of lawless men did crucify and slay: whom God raised up, having loosed the pangs of death.'[1]

There can then, be little doubt that the resurrection of Jesus was regarded by the early Christians as full and complete confirmation that Jesus was the Christ: it was the belief in the resurrection which in their eyes entirely justified the complete re-interpretation of the traditional Jewish conception of Messiahship and enabled them to see the hand of God in the birth, call, ministry and shameful death of the man Jesus of Nazareth.

The New Testament tradition of the Ascension of Christ is found in the Acts of the Apostles and in the closing verses of St. Luke's Gospel. As St. Mark's Gospel now ends it contains a simple reference to the Ascension:[2] St. Matthew and St. John make no reference to it. St. Luke's account, however, is particularly interesting and may be quoted in full as it stands in the English (Revised) Version:

'And he led them out until they were over against

---

[1] Acts ii. 23-24; cf. iii. 15; iv. 10-11.
[2] It is universally agreed that verses 9-20 of the present Ch. 16 were not part of its original conclusion.

Bethany: and he lifted up his hands and blessed them. And it came to pass while he blessed them, he parted from them, and was carried up into heaven. And they worshipped him, and returned to Jerusalem with great joy: and were continually in the temple, blessing God.'[1]

In two ancient MSS., namely a version of the Codex Sinaiticus and in the Codex Bezae, together with two ancient versions (Old Latin and one form of the Syriac) and in some of St. Augustine's quotations, the words 'and was carried up into heaven' are omitted.[2] While there are quite a considerable number of important MSS. which include these words, the disagreement is not without significance: it suggests that the traditional account of the Ascension presented difficulties even to some of the early Christians. Exactly what those difficulties were it is not easy to imagine; they could hardly have arisen out of an uneasiness about a crude spacial conception of 'heaven', for this notion would probably have been widely accepted. It is more likely that from the very beginning there had been difficulty in agreeing on a precise description of the events which marked the conclusion of the experience underlying the 'resurrection appearances' and the beginning of a new stage in the experience of the early followers of Christ.

However this may be, it is at any rate clear that the dominant tradition included the belief that Christ ascended visibly to heaven. Such a conception would no doubt have seemed to most of the early Christians the proper and fitting ending to the earthly ministry of Christ and prelude to his session 'at the right hand of

---

[1] Luke xxiv. 50-53.
[2] So also are the words 'and they worshipped him' omitted from the same texts—except this time for the Codex Sinaiticus, which includes them.

God'. The notion would have been a familiar one to Jewish Christians: Enoch was believed in later Jewish tradition to have been taken up to heaven without dying[1] and Elijah mounted up to heaven in a chariot of fire.

[1] See Heb. xi. 5.

NINETEEN

THE CHRIST

Just as the emerging of a definite 'Buddhology' is evident in the canonical scriptures of Buddhism, so the beginnings of a formulated Christology can be seen in the New Testament. The subject has been discussed exhaustively in a number of able works and all that is necessary here is to summarise rather than to attempt a full discussion of, the New Testament views of the person of Christ. For this purpose we must notice three main streams of thought—the Pauline, the Johannine and that of the Epistle to the Hebrews—in which the main Christological conclusions of the early Christians find expression.

St. Paul's Epistles cover the period approximately from A.D. 50 to 64 and therefore furnish us with valuable evidence for the development of Christological belief in the Churches influenced by St. Paul's teaching during this period. Dr. Rawlinson, in *The New Testament Doctrine of the Christ*, frankly recognises a development in St. Paul's thought of the person of Christ. As it came to him originally, the earlier and general interpretation seems to have been that Jesus was Messiah; it was in the capacity of a Jewish claimant to Messiahship that he went to his crucifixion. As a result of the development of the belief in his resurrection and ascension, the early Christians seem to have believed further that Jesus would return in the near future as the exalted Messiah, the Son of Man of apocalyptic tradition, coming on the clouds as he had gone up on them.[1] To what extent this latter belief was fully developed when St. Paul's influence

[1] See e.g. Acts i. 11.

upon Christian teaching began to be exerted, and how far its importance was the outcome of St. Paul's own work, is by no means clear. It is, however, quite clear from the Epistles to the Thessalonians and to the Corinthians that St. Paul fully accepted it, though Corinthians seems to indicate that he was already beginning to feel the need for certain modifications of its earlier forms.[1]

As we have already noticed, St. Paul introduces the idea of Christ's pre-existence and he seems to have reached this conception by connecting the ideas of Christ as the 'Heavenly Man' of apocalyptic literature and as the 'image of God'.[2] At the same time, his Sonship is read back into the past, so that he pre-exists from all eternity with God, as His 'Son'.[3]

It is possible to attempt to trace the path by which St. Paul came to such conclusions. It is evident that Christ was to St. Paul the true and only surviving human representative of the chosen people to whom the promises were made. In Romans he develops this theme and tries to show that whereas the sphere of those promises had been narrowed down by sin to one man only, through the work of redemption which had become available for all men without qualification, the promises had become universally available.[4] He then seems gradually to have moved from the thought of the greatness of the universal redemption to the thought of the greatness of the personal agent of God through whom it was possible, and concluded that as 'God was in Christ reconciling the world unto himself', so God had 'highly exalted' the Redeemer and 'gave unto him the name which is above every name'.[5]

---

[1] Cf. I Cor. xv with 1 Thess. iv. 13-18.
[2] Cf. 1 Cor. xv. 49; 2 Cor. iv. 4; Col. i. 15; Quick, however, does not accept Rawlinson's view here; see *Doctrines of the Creed*, p. 82, note 1; Lond. 1938.
[3] Phil. ii. 5-11.   [4] Rom. 3-11.   [5] Phil. ii. 9-10.

St. Paul's Christology may therefore be seen to begin with the conception of the human Messiah and to have passed from the thought of the greatness of the redemption wrought by him as God's agent to that of the unique character of the Redeemer himself. Whether St. Paul however, actually reached the point at which he identified Christ with God seems very doubtful. There is no clear evidence that he actually used the name '$\theta\epsilon\acute{o}s$' (God) of Christ, though there seems little doubt that, in Canon Quick's words, 'St. Paul did definitely, if one may be allowed the expression, rank Jesus with God.'[1]

The Epistle to the Hebrews reflects a similar development but it takes a slightly different form. Christ is there primarily the 'Great High Priest' who by the sacrifice of himself has consecrated for the people of God 'a new and living way'. The imagery used is that of the temple and the sacrificial system; Christ has been revealed as the true 'High Priest' who offers the true and perfect sacrifice by the shedding of his own blood and so has made it possible for men to enter 'with boldness' into 'the holy place'.[2]

This redemption by blood-shedding has, however, been wrought by one who is perfect man. He is a high priest that can be 'touched with the feeling of our infirmities . . . one that hath been in all points tempted like as we are, yet without sin.'[3] And again, as the 'captain of their salvation', he was made 'perfect through sufferings', and 'having been made perfect, he became unto all them that obey him the captain of eternal salvation.'[4]

Nevertheless, as with St. Paul, so evidently with the author of Hebrews, the greatness and uniqueness of the

---

[1] *Doctrines of the Creed*, p. 83.
[2] Heb. x. 19-25; cf. ix. 11 ff.
[3] Heb. iv. 15.
[4] Heb. ii. 10 and v. 9.

redemption wrought led to the thought of the greatness and uniqueness of the redeemer, and was connected with the thought of his pre-existence with God from the beginning. So the Son is he whom God 'appointed heir of all things, through whom also he made the worlds; who being the effulgence of his glory, and the very image of his substance, and upholding all things by the word of his power, when he had made purification of sins, sat down on the right hand of the Majesty on high; having become by so much better than the angels, as he hath inherited a more excellent name than they.'[1]

The writer brings both the humanity and the divinity of Christ together in connection with the imagery of the temple veil. The eternal Son came forth from the 'heavenward' side of the veil which separates God from men and having wrought man's redemption and having thus reconciled man to God, returns through the veil again and in so doing paves the way for his redeemed brethren to follow.[2]

The Christology of the Gospel and Epistles of St. John represents an approach from a quite opposite point of view to that of St. Paul and the author of Hebrews. We have already seen that for St. John the significant truth about Christ is that he is first and foremost the incarnate Son of God. The earthly life of Jesus is a declaration of Divine truth and we somehow get the impression that the Son of God never, in a sense, really left the Father's side. The belief in the atonement is reached through the belief in the incarnation, whereas in St. Paul and Hebrews, as we have noticed, the thought of the atonement leads on and up to the thought of the incarnation. Whereas to St. Paul, and even to the author of Hebrews, the earthly life of Jesus is the supremely

[1] Heb. i. 2-4.   [2] Heb. x. 19-20; ix. 24.

effective act of God's love, to St. John it is its uniquely true symbol or expression.[1]

It must not, however, be imagined that in thus stressing the revelational character of Christ's humanity, St. John in any way suggests that that humanity was not fully real. One of the main concerns of the writer was to combat precisely that sort of 'docetic' belief which had obviously begun to manifest itself in certain forms of gnostic teaching. Thus he declares that 'The Word became flesh', and that 'Word of Life' they have heard, seen with their eyes, beheld, and handled with their hands. Again, the test of the 'spirits' which are 'of God' is that they confess 'that Jesus Christ is come in the flesh'.[2] Thus, though St. John puts the primary emphasis upon the divinity of Christ, he ends, as St. Paul and the author of Hebrews do, by stressing the common traditional Christian view that Christ embodies in himself both divinity and perfect humanity. This is, in fact, the plain declaration of the New Testament as a whole: the man Jesus is the Christ, and as the Christ of God he is also the pre-existent, divine Son of God. At the same time it must be recognised that this is the limit of the New Testament Christology. There is no attempt at solving the problems raised by the assertion of Christ's perfect humanity and of his divinity; there is not even recognition that any problems exist. Both that recognition and attempts at a solution were part of the task which later generations of Christian thinkers had to face.

[1] See e.g. John i. 18; xiv. 9; xiv. 31, etc.
[2] John i. 14; 1 John i. 1; 1 John iv. 2.

TWENTY

SOME REFLECTIONS

The fact that within these three groups of sacred writings it is possible to find passages like those here quoted which in each case and in various ways reflect the view—and in some places explicitly state—that the Founder of the Faith manifested in himself supernatural qualities and characteristics raises, of course, a number of profound and difficult questions. In the limited space left to us here little more can be done than to note these questions and to indicate the directions in which possible answers to them might lead.

Obviously the first question which will be asked is whether the three sets of sacred traditions do actually arrive at views of the supernatural character of the Founder which are fundamentally similar, or at any rate similar enough to justify their being grouped together. On the face of it, we could hardly expect to find a close identity either of theological view-point or of language. The centuries-old religious thought of the Far East has proceeded along different lines from that of either the Near Middle East or the Mediterranean world and while Buddhism was a child of Far Eastern religious experience, Islam and Christianity took their rise amidst that of the Near Middle East and the Mediterranean world. In Buddhist scriptures we may trace two distinct streams of thought about Buddha's divinity. When viewed against the background of the gods of the Hindu pantheon he is 'the god beyond the gods'. In the full Mahāyāna view, however, the further stage is reached at which the Buddha is identified with ultimate reality: his historical manifestation as Sākyamuni is but one aspect of the essential Buddha-nature which ultimately is to be thought of as the Absolute.

At first sight there appears to be a close resemblance between the Mahāyāna view of the supernatural character of the Buddha and the view of Christ as the Word made flesh in St. John's writings in the New Testament and various writers have in fact drawn such an analogy. There is, however, an important difference between these two ideas. Christianity had inherited from Judaism a monotheistic conception of ultimate reality and this inevitably led to a view of the form of Christ's divinity different from that of the divinity of the Buddha. The Christ whose unique character as the personal agent in God's great redemptive plan for mankind had so impressed St. Paul and the writer of the Epistle to the Hebrews was not identified with God in a monistic sense but was said to be 'Son of God'—a relationship which might be taken to be suggestive of subordination to God but which, as later Christological controversy made clear, was in fact interpreted to mean that he was 'of the same substance as' the Father. Allowing, however, for this important difference it can fairly be said that both in Buddhism and in Christianity the way was found to express the idea of the fundamental oneness of the Founder with ultimate reality.

In the case of Islam, though there are clear signs of a movement towards this same idea, it cannot be said to have been actually reached. Much more investigation needs to be done before any clear opinion can be formed on this whole subject but in the present state of our knowledge it seems fair to suggest that two distinguishable movements of ideas about the person of the Prophet can be distinguished within the Qur'an and the Traditions. On the one hand there are the signs, of which we have taken note, that a spontaneous veneration of the Prophet quickly grew among his followers. On the other, there was a denite theological development inspired particularly by the Shī'īs which, starting from the idea that a manifestation of the divine was present in the Prophet and handed on to his true successors, led eventually to a belief in the Prophet's pre-existence. The idea of the Prophet as 'The Light of Allāh' and so as the first individuation of the Divine Essence, is a further stage in this same theological development. It will be clear that this particular manner of expressing the special relationship of the Prophet to Allāh does not rise to the same theological level as is the case with the doctrines of the Buddha and of the Christ. That it did not do so may well have been due to the fact that the Shī'a theologians adhered firmly to the belief that the main form of the revelation of Allāh to mankind was in the eternal and uncreated Qur'an. Indeed, viewed in the light of this last article of faith, it is remarkable that the doctrine of the person of the Prophet proceeded even as far as it did.

A provisional and tentative answer to our first question then, would seem to be that there is not a complete identity, either of content or of form, in the traditional ascription of supernatural character to the Buddha, the Prophet and the Christ. There is, however, an attempt on the part of all three traditions to associate the Founder in a special sense with ultimate reality. In Buddhism and in Christianity this association is finally reached and clearly expressed: in Islam a similar process of thought is seen at work but the full association does not seem to have taken place.

A further question of some importance which arises directly from that which has just been considered is whether this attempt to ascribe to the Founder supernatural qualities and character is regarded in each case as equally important in and central to the fundamental gospel of these three religions. In dealing with a problem of this kind it is possible to indulge in dangerous generalisations about the devotional attitudes of adherents of the three Faiths which could in the nature of the case hold good only for certain groups within them. Each is a religion which has attracted followers of many different types, whose interpretations of the Faith have necessarily been varied. Confining the question then, as far as possible to the main theological tradition in each case, it seems clear that in Mahāyāna Buddhism and in Christianity the close association of the Founder with ultimate reality is generally regarded as an essential element in the religion itself. In the Mahāyāna the faith and adoration of the Buddhist disciple is centred not upon the historical Sākyamuni but upon the eternal Buddha who, in 'The Lotus of the Good Law' is pictured as saying:

'I see the utter destruction of men, and yet I do not show them my own form. But if perchance they yearn to see me, I expound the Good Law to those who thirst for it.'

The attitude of the Fourth Gospel is closely akin, as when St. Thomas is made to ask Jesus to show them the Father and is told: 'He that hath seen me hath seen the Father.'

Moreover, in the sense in which we have seen that the beginnings of the Buddhology of the Mahāyāna are to be found in the Hīnayāna it is possible to take the view that our conclusion must hold good for the Hīnayāna also. It must, however, be remembered that the Hīnayāna has continued to exist in certain countries in forms which appear to have remained largely unaffected by the full Mahāyāna developments. This type of Buddhism would seem to place less emphasis upon the Buddha as an object of faith and adoration and more upon the value of following the Path along which he first led the way. At the same time we have noticed how even here his followers naturally tended to regard him with feelings of particular respect, affection and of veneration—a fact which makes it difficult to say even of the Hīnayāna, that the idea of the supernatural character of the Buddha is of no significance.

The case of Islam is again somewhat complicated. We have seen that popular veneration of the Prophet figures to no small degree in the theological ideas of certain forms of Islam. We have also noticed that at a very early stage in the life of Islam the Prophet was venerated increasingly by his followers. Again, the idea of the heavenly intercession of the Prophet is particularly deep-rooted in Muslim theology and so—though perhaps to a lesser degree—is the belief in his pre-existence. It is manifestly difficult in these circumstances to argue that a purely human conception of the Prophet is adequate for a proper interpretation even of Sunni beliefs. The Shī'a interpretation, as we have already noted, involves a doctrine of the person of the Prophet in which supernatural characteristics play an even more important part.

To this question, therefore, it is difficult to give a precise answer. Perhaps the most that can be said is that it is difficult to see how a purely human interpretation of the person of the Founder could satisfy any of the main stages of religious thought in Buddhism, Islam or Christianity, while in the fully-developed Buddhology and Christology of the Mahāyāna and Christianity respectively the close association of the Founder with ultimate reality becomes an essential element of the Faith.

The tentative answers given to these two enquiries inevitably raise a further problem, namely whether the persistent tendency in these three religious traditions to regard the Founder as manifesting in himself more than purely human qualities and characteristics, and in some instances as being associated in a special manner with ultimate reality itself, is to be traced to the possibility that there has been a process of 'borrowing' of ideas. That is to say, have the ideas which originally formed part of the beliefs of one of the three religions found their way into the other two and so brought about the similarities which we have noticed?

It may be said at once that there has not been any serious attempt on the part of scholars to suggest that such borrowing has occurred as between Buddhism and Islam. A good deal of attention has, however, been given to the possible influence on the one hand of Christianity upon Buddhism—or vice versa—and on the other of Christianity upon Islam. These again, are large questions and nothing more than a summary of the general consensus of opinion on them can be given here.

That some sort of contacts between Middle and Far Eastern peoples were made—particularly following the conquests of Alexander the Great—seems fairly certain. It is well known, for example, that Clement of Alexandria, the Christian philosopher and theologian (fl. c. A.D. 200) refers in his 'Stromata' to the followers of 'Boutta' (Buddha),[1] and Lloyd has gone as far as to suggest that certain resemblances between some forms of heretical Christian teaching found in Alexandria and Buddhist beliefs indicate that 'there must have been in circulation in Alexandria, during the latter half of the first century A.D., a Buddhist book or collection of books which was the "Ur-evangelium" of several heresies.' He has also suggested that the early Christian legend, given in the Apocryphal Acts of St. Thomas, and supported by

[1] Stromata I. 15.

the testimony of Eusebius and others, which connects the Apostle Thomas with the valley of the Indus, is at least so far true in its earlier part 'that there actually was Christian preaching at a very early period in North-West India.'[1] It must also be remembered that Alexandria and Antioch were both centres of vigorous Christian life and also centres of trade with the Orient and that an exchange of Buddhist and Christian ideas and even of documents must therefore be regarded as at least a possibility. However, all this, interesting and suggestive as it is, does not amount to solid evidence and we are left at present with the general conclusion that, so far as Buddhism and Christianity are concerned, while it is possible that the existence of some teaching of the Buddha may have become known in certain parts of the Christian world by the end of the second century A.D., the external evidence so far available does not indicate that any serious influence was exerted by the one upon the other until well after the content and the form of the respective scriptures had been settled.

The internal evidence for a literary connection between the Buddhist and Christian traditions has been reviewed to some extent by Thomas.[2] There are quite striking parallels which have understandably given rise to the argument that one tradition has influenced the other. In both Buddhist and Christian scriptures we have noticed stories of the miraculous birth of the Founder, of his presentation to a holy man, of his temptation, of his transfiguration, and of miracles, including that of the disciple walking on the water. If, however, Dr. Law's conclusions as to the dates of the formation of the Pāli canon are accepted, it seems clear that on the whole any

[1] *The Creed of Half Japan*, Chs. VII and VIII; Lond. 1911. The Acts of Thomas are translated into English and may be referred to in Dr. M. R. James' edition of *The Apocryphal Gospels*, pp. 364-438; Oxf. 1924.
[2] See *The Life of Buddha*, Ch. XVII.

suggestion of the Pāli writings having been influenced by the Christian scriptures must be ruled out, for it would appear that the final form of the Pāli canon was fixed before the end of the first century B.C.[1] It is, of course, just possible that the reverse process operated and that the Christian scriptures were influenced by the Pāli but on the one hand there is no evidence to support such a conclusion and on the other it has to be remembered that the miraculous events connected with the birth, life and death of Christ are so numerous that it is difficult to single out three or four as evidence of possible literary dependence of Christianity upon Buddhism. Similarly there is a not inconsiderable number of Buddhist miracle-stories that have no parallel in the Christian tradition. Were the alleged parallelisms much greater in number, such an argument would need to be considered more seriously.

When we turn to the question of the contacts between Islam and Christianity we are confronted with a more definite situation. It is generally agreed that the Prophet himself had some knowledge, even if he did not understand the more normal interpretation of, such Christian beliefs as those of the Virgin Birth and the Resurrection of Jesus. We have also noted the possibility that in the period during which Tradition was evolving there may well have been a tendency for Muslims to claim for their Prophet a status not inferior to that afforded by the Christians to Christ. There is also to be borne in mind the important fact that during the period of the Umaiyad Caliphs (c. A.D. 660-750) there was considerable intercourse between Muslim and Christian apologists and theologians. In the face of this accumulation of evidence there can be no doubt about the fact that Christian ideas have played a part in helping to shape the development

[1] See pp. 17-18.

of certain aspects of Muslim theology, including ideas about the person of the Prophet. At the same time it must be recognised that there is little evidence to suggest that this influence of the Muslim sacred traditions by the Christian is to be construed as a mere plagiarising on the part of either Muhammad or of the Traditionists. Islamic beliefs form a *corpus* and are expressive of the whole gospel and spirit of Islam and are not simply a loose admixture of Arabian, Jewish and Christian ideas.

These brief comments would be incomplete without at least a reference to a quite different kind of attempt to explain part, at any rate, of the resemblances we have been considering. It was put forward by Dibelius in his *Die Formgeschichte des Evangeliums* already referred to and suggests that many similarities between the Buddhist and Christian stories of miraculous happenings in connection with the traditions of the life and teaching of the Founders are to be traced, at any rate in the forms in which we now have them, to the operation of a 'law of biographical analogy'. Dibelius says:

'We could almost speak of *a law of biographical analogy* which is to be seen here. At bottom is to be found a fixed idea of the life of a holy man: such a man may neither be born nor die without the significance of the event being proclaimed from heaven. His future calling is announced even in his youth, and in the same way his end throws its shadows in advance. Divine powers are always ready to help him in stress and to proclaim his merits. Many points of agreement between the Buddha-legends and the Jesus-legends, as well as between Christian Apostle- and saint-legends arise, not from borrowing, but from this law of biographical analogy leading to formulations constantly renewed.'[1]

[1] pp. 108-109 in English translation.

This theory is at least striking and original and would, if correct, provide a possible explanation of many of the similarities which we have noticed in the Buddhist and Christian traditions. Presumably it could be extended to account also for some of the similarities between them and the Islamic tradition.

In the last resort, however, the significance of the facts which emerge from these selections from the three sacred traditions must seem even more important than possible explanations of their origin. The fact must not, of course, be lost sight of that the ways in which each of these three religions interprets the nature of ultimate reality and the path by which men can ultimately attain to an understanding of and union with it are by no means identical. Even more necessary is it to recognise, however, that underlying these divergences is to be found a spiritual approach to the problem of the meaning of human life, the significance of which is profoundly important at a time when men are anxiously searching for firmer foundations upon which to base a respect for those moral and spiritual values which are seen to be essential if the age of science is not to become the prelude to a new era of barbarism. It is not merely that these three religions unite in declaring that materialism, whether old or new, is inadequate as a philosophy of a life which can be fully understood only in terms of a transcendent, spiritual purpose: that belief we have the right to expect to find at the root of all developed religion. They also agree, however, in declaring that this spiritual purpose has been revealed to mankind by—and even in—one who manifests in himself in a special way ultimate reality itself. Man, they declare, has not been left to struggle alone towards this all-important truth; his efforts have met with an issuing-forth from ultimate reality itself. To use, for a moment, in this wider context the imagery which

St. John applied to the effect of the Christian revelation: the eternal light has shined in the darkness of human frailty and perplexity. In a day when men are acutely conscious both of that frailty and of that perplexity they need, above all, to be drawn into that light. That they should thus begin to see things temporal in the light of things eternal is, for our day and generation, the most pressing need of all and here, at all events, these three great Faiths can speak with one voice.

Behold, I show you Truth! Lower than hell
Higher than heaven, outside the utmost stars,
   Farther than Brahm doth dwell,

Before beginning, and without an end,
   As space eternal and as surety sure,
Is fixed a Power divine which moves to good,
   Only its laws endure.

This is its work upon the things ye see:
   The unseen things are more; men's hearts and minds,
The thoughts of peoples and their ways and wills,
   Those too, the great Law binds.

Such is the Law which moves to righteousness,
   Which none at last can turn aside or stay;
The heart of it is Love, the end of it
   Is Peace and Consummation sweet. . . .
        (From Sir Edwin Arnold's *The Light of Asia*).

INDEX

Abū Bakr, 97, 98, 107
Abū Dāwūd, 73
Abū Hurairah, 111
Abū Jahl, 96
Acts of Apostles, 148
Ālavī, 44
Alexander the Great, 161
Ali, 109
Amina, 83, 84
Ānanda, 17, 45, 48ff
Anesaki, 29n
Anuruddha, 51
Arahant, 22
Arberry, 79n
Arnold. E., 166
Asita, 26
Asoka, 15, 17
Asvaghosha, 65
Augustine. St., 149
Awakening of Faith, 65, 67
Āyishah, 106, 108n

Badr, Battle of, 100
Al-Baghawī, 75
Bath ḳol, 139
Bethmann, 79n, 80
Blunt, 135n
Bodhisattva, 64 and n
Buddhaghosa, 16
Buhksh, 88n
Al-Bukhārī, 72-73
Bultmann, 143

Cave, 58n
Cicero, 132
Civa, 57
Clement of Alexandria, 161
Codex Bezae, 149
Codex Sinaiticus, 149 and n
Conze, 11

Councils, Buddhist, 17f
Cullavagga, 41
Cunda, the Great, 43
Cunda, the smith, 50

Deva, 57
Dibelius, 123, 143-144, 164-165
Dodd, 123n

Edmunds, 30n
Elijah, 150
Enoch, 150

Form Criticism, 123-4, 143-4

Gabriel, 78, 85, 86, 87, 88, 92ff, 107-8, 113, 129
Gaudefroy-Demombynes, 112
Gibb, 116-7
Grandmaison, 145
Guillaume, 72, 73, 75n, 103-4, 104n, 116

Hādith, 71-5
Hadnibiah, Battle of, 102
Al-hallāj, 117
Hebrews, Ep. to, 125-6, 150, 153-4
Hijrah, 92, 97
Hinduism, 21
Horner, 39

Ibn Isḥāk, 79
Ibn Mādjā, 73
Imāmate, 78
Intercession, of Muhammed, 91, 110ff
isnād, 74

James, E. O., 58n
James, M. R., 162
John's, St. Gosp. and Eps., 126, 135, 136n, 146, 148, 154–5, 157, 159, 166
Josephus, 121
Junjirō, 60–1

Kāladevala, 29
Kanishka, 17
Kanthaka, 33
Kapilavatthu, 20
karma, 21–2
Kassapa, 43, 51
Kathāvatthu, 52n, 54–6
Keith, 52n, 57–8, 61, 64n
Khadīja, 87, 89
Al-Kindī, 103, 104
Kirk, 139
Knox, W. L., 131
Koelle, 76, 80, 81n, 82, 83n, 84, 94 and n, 108n, 109n, 110n, 115
Kosala, 15
Al-Kulīnī, 75
Kusinārā, 50

Lalita-vistara, 31
Law, B. C., 17–18, 30, 162–3
Lewis, C. S., 140
Light of Muhammad, 77f
Lion roar, 47
Lloyd, 63, 161
Lotus of the Good Law, 67–8, 159
Luke, St., 129–130, 132, 134, 135–6, 147, 148–9

Magadha, 15
Malalasekera, 20n
Māra, 35–38, 48, 89–90
Margoliouth, 90, 102n, 115–6
Mark, St., 134, 136, 138, 148 and n
Matthew, St., 128–9, 132–3, 134, 146, 148
Māyā, Queen, 20

McGovern, 20n
Medina, 98, 102, 109, 112
Milinda Pañha, 18
Mishkātu, 75 *et al.*
Mogallāna, 33
Muir, 73, 88n, 98n, 102n, 106n, 107n, 108n
Muslim, the Traditionist, 73
Mutazilites, 112

Nargajuna, 19
Al-Nasā'ī, 73
Niddesa, 57
Night-Journey of Muhammad, 92ff
Night of Power, 86 and n, 88
nirvāna, 44, 46, 49n, 51, 68
North, 76n

Oldenberg, 60
Oral Tradition (Buddhist), 16
Oral Tradition (New Testament), 123
Othman, 71

Pāli, 15ff
Pātaliputta, 17
Patna, 65
Paul, St., 68, 126–7, 127n, 151ff, 157
Philippians, Ep. to, 125
Pliny, 121
Pratt, 58n, 68
Pukkusa, 45

qadar, 113 and n
Qastalānī, Imām, 77
Quick, O., 152n, 153
Qur'an, 71
Qur'an (quoted), 85–88, 89n, 90, 92, 95–6, 97n, 101, 110–111

Rāhula, 32
Rājagaha, 17
Ramaḍān, 86n

Rawlinson, 127n, 128, 151, 152n
Relics, of Buddha, 52
Report on Doctrine in Church of England, 130–131
Rhys Davids, Mrs., 60 and n
Rhys Davids, Prof., 48
Richardson, A., 140, 142n, 143,4,5
Rodwell, 92n, 110n

Sākyamuni, 63, 68, 159
Sāriputta, 47
Satan, 89 and n, 101, 135
Saunders, 58n
Sell, 79n, 96n, 111–12
Shī'a, 74, 5, 6, 7, 8, 9, 80n, 116–7, 158, 160
Son of Man, 151–2
Sonadanda, 58
Splitting of Moon, 96
Steinilber-Oberlin, 19, 68n
Suetonius, 132
Sūfīs, 78–9
Suzuki, Mrs., 19, 64ff
Sweetman, 77–8, 103n, 111n, 113

Al-Ṭabarī, 104
Tacitus, 121
Tasker, 123n
Taylor, Vincent, 123, 131n
Theragāthā, 39
Thomas, E. J., 20n, 25–6, 38, 42n, 44n, 45n, 52n, 57n, 58, 162
Al-Tirmidhī, 73
Tīssa, 44
Tor Andrae, 79n
Trīkaya doctrine, 64ff, 157
Tusita heaven, 20

Umaiyad Caliphs, 163
Upāli, 17
Upavāna, 50

Vimānavatthu, 33
Virgil, 132
Virgin Birth, 128ff
Viṣṇu, 57
Visvāmitra, 31
Al-Wāḳidī, 87, 92, 97

Zwemer, 94, 112n, 118